A Rainbow in the Dark

Colleen Sullivan Clapper

ISBN: 978-0-578-28463-7 (Paperback)
ISBN: 978-0-578-28462-0 (E-book)

Library of Congress Control Number: 2022909497

Front cover photo by Tim O'Malley and design by Jessica Chew.

First printing edition 2022.

To contact Colleen, go to: https://www.realandrawministry.org or email her at Blueprint4u@gmail.com

This book is dedicated to my husband, Jim. You are my soulmate, best friend, main prayer partner, editor, and co-writer in a chapter. You have literally saved my life multiple times, make me laugh, are the best kisser, one of the most righteous people I know, and I can go on and on. I couldn't have written this book without you. I pray we walk by one another forever and stop the world until we melt!

CONTENTS

Introduction vii

Important Note xiii

Chapter 1 Your Brilliant & Unique Purpose 1

Chapter 2 Community & Fellowship 19

Chapter 3 Unanswered Prayers 31

Chapter 4 Eternal Perspective 45

Chapter 5 Don't Give Up! Navy Seal Kind Of Thinking....59

Chapter 6 Spiritual Depression, Joy, & Hope 79

Chapter 7 Rest, Restoration, & Redemption 91

Chapter 8 God's Love...107

Chapter 9 Love Annihilates Evil.. 117

Chapter 10 Encouragement 127

Chapter 11 Better Than A Fairytale Ending 145

INTRODUCTION

To shake the hand of someone who has been beaten near to death is a humbling experience. To know that person suffered for his or her faith makes it even more powerful. I have experienced this kind of meeting numerous times. These survivors have endured the darkness of persecution, yet each explained that the oppression of the mind is worse than the beatings. It wasn't just the physical torment that caused them to despair at times, but the mind games they endured. They believe we all experience these darkest hours at one time or another and frequently for some. The more I go through life and the more people I meet, I truly believe that everyone does struggle with pain, loss, fear, anger, injustice, etc. We all go through times when our world seems to crash around us, and we can barely function. So, how can we deal with all of that darkness? How does the rainbow appear in the dark? Where can we find hope to face the day?

Rainbows require light. So, thinking of a rainbow appearing in the dark seems impossible. Yet, this book will show that it *is* possible. I've seen it. I have seen a rainbow in the dark. It has taken personal hardship to understand the possibility of deeper hope and joy. I have been on the floor, crying out to God to take away the pain. There have been times I haven't wanted to get out of bed, let alone pray. Even still, God promises to be that Light, that rainbow in the dark. "If I say, 'Surely the darkness will hide me, and the light will become night around me,' even the darkness will not be dark to you; the night will shine like the day, for darkness is as light to you" (Psalm 139:11-12 NIV).

When Jim and I were first married, I quickly learned the difference between a "night owl" and an "early bird," much to my dismay. I love staying up late, but I also love sleeping in. So, nothing could have prepared me for Jim singing "Zippity Do Da" and whistling upon waking up. I was waiting for birds to fly in our bedroom window and mice to start cleaning our apartment, but instead, I would pull the covers over my head (admittedly, I found it somewhat entertaining). Some mornings, though, have not been so joyful. As mentioned, there have been mornings when I didn't want to get out of bed, let alone pray—and I didn't know how I could be an encouragement to others when I, myself, was so discouraged.

I've spoken on the topic of profound discouragement locally, nationally, and internationally. Interestingly, when I ask audiences how many of them did not want to get out of bed that morning (not due to being tired), the majority of the people raise their hands. At first, the number of raised hands surprised me, but it doesn't anymore. This is a universal condition. Never have I had such a long list of prayer requests or known so many people going through multiple major trials all at once. We are in difficult and trying times.

The morning after being date raped, I felt such unjustified guilt that I wanted to hide underneath the covers permanently. After our daughter died, there were mornings when the emotions were so intense that I didn't want to wake up and experience it again. There are mornings, due to my disability, when the pain is so strong that I'm not sure how making it through the day will be possible. I write about these experiences in detail in my book *The Raindrops on the Windshield Sound Like Popcorn.*

After reading my first book, people would say to me that I have great faith. Missionary James Hudson Taylor exclaimed, "You do not need a great faith, but faith in a great God."[1]

We don't forge ahead by our strength alone. God is the one who gives me the strength to get out of bed! Again, my first book was about some of the trials my family and I have endured. God used that book to open many doors, about which you will read in this book.

I was asked to speak twice in a tribal prison in the Southwest United States. People have read my book in Africa and India. I had the opportunity to work with the Maasai (an ethnic group from Kenya and northern Tanzania) and with those with special abilities. I was invited to speak at a church in Poland that serves Holocaust survivors and at a church in Canada that is primarily facilitated by those with special abilities. There were even more adventures, and each time I was able to meet more of God's wonderful people. I have learned from each experience and am grateful. I pray that this book opens more doors and more opportunities, but most of all, I hope you will find inspiration to not just survive but to thrive through your own times of discouragement and trials. It is through sharing our personal experiences or learning the stories of others that we can learn to see the rainbow in the dark.

I love a summer's night when you can sit outside sipping on lemonade and listen to big band music while gazing at the stars and lightning bugs. The stars and the lightning bugs become brighter as the night grows darker. That's what faith is like. Light shines brighter when it's darkest. "This is the message we have heard from him and declare to you: God is light; in him there is no darkness at all" (1 John 1:5 NIV).

Rainbows need light. When we are tired, we can see God's love and faithfulness even more and grow closer to Him. God is The Rainbow in the dark. He will never leave our side and constantly holds us in His everlasting light.

Therefore, since we have been justified through faith, we have peace with God through our Lord Jesus Christ, through whom we have gained access by faith into this grace in which we now stand. And we boast in the hope of the glory of God. Not only so, but we also glory in our sufferings, because we know that suffering produces perseverance; perseverance, character; and character, hope. And hope does not put us to shame, because God's love has been poured out into our hearts through the Holy Spirit, who has been given to us. (Romans 5:1-5 NIV)

Endnotes

1   Roger Steer, Hudson Taylor: Lessons in Discipleship (OMF International, 1995), 51, as found at https://quotepark.com/authors/james-hudson-taylor.

IMPORTANT NOTE

∾

I am aware that using references from the Bible may not resonate with those who don't believe that it is the inspired Word of God. I would like to explain why I do. First, the Bible was written on three continents by over forty authors from diverse ethnic and occupational backgrounds in three different languages over 1,600 years. Even so, the message is consistent from start to finish. It answers the questions of life and death, sin and redemption, purpose, and our place in the universe, making it a unified book not from forty different minds but the mind of our Maker, the God of gods. Second, there are more ancient copies of biblical texts than any other work in history. Third, the plethora of translations that have been made from the original Greek, Hebrew, and Aramaic provide proof that the versions we read today are 99.5 percent accurate to the originals.

I have experienced God's written Word to be the Truth in my life again and again. There is no doubt in my mind that it is God's love letter to us.

CHAPTER 1

YOUR BRILLIANT & UNIQUE PURPOSE

∼❧∼

I can see you and hear you repeating my name, but I can't get my mouth to move. My arms and legs won't move either. Wait, my arm is starting to thrash on its own. I feel like an alien. Everything seems so surreal. My thoughts are all jumbled, flashing images of the past, present, and now the grocery list in my mind. I know what I want to say, but are they the right words? I see the looks in your eyes and even the tears forming. Yes, that's what I want to tell you . . . to let you know, I will be okay. Do I even believe that? For the most part, there is always that fear that I will become permanently paralyzed this time. Come on, lungs, don't stop now. Focus . . . breath in, breath out. Remember the article I just read . . . it said new neurons can be formed. God, can you override this and heal me? If it's not your will to heal me completely right now, can you give me strength? Or is it my time?

I am not afraid of death. I know what's next; peace, joy, and no more tears. It would eliminate the stress on my loved ones.

Maybe I can close my eyes and slip away. No, Jim is telling me I can make it. He is saying he needs me here. Does he know how much his love gives me strength? Do all my kids, grandchildren, and loved ones understand that they help to keep me going? Why does God allow this to happen? Why the pain? But this does draw me closer to Him because I realize I am only breathing because of Him. And I want to stay here. I want to see my grandbabies grow up and other amazing events still to come. I still want to dance in as many countries as possible, and there are several I haven't been to yet. I still have hope. Right now, I need the muscles to release in my neck. I am on . . . what number? Yes, count one, two, three . . . my fifteenth seizure in a row. I am so tired. Very tired. Come on, I can do this. Silence. I feel myself coming back, and I can mumble slurred words. It's a humbling victory . . . realizing life, once again, is so fragile.

- My thoughts during one of my seizures a few years ago.

As much as I've hated my medical complications, they've taught me to embrace life. I love the quote from Joyce Meyer stating: "Having a rough morning? Place your hand over your heart . . . feel that? That's called purpose. You're alive for a reason. Don't give up." As mentioned in the Introduction, there are days when many of us don't want to get out of bed. As I'm working on this chapter, the snowflakes are coming down gracefully but in a frenzy. I'm still in my robe, and it's 2:17 p.m. It's one of those stay home days.

I've had many of these days and have been on bedrest several times. It's at these times that I begin to question my purpose. Am I making a difference in the world? I'm pretty sure we all do this at times. Yet, look at the stats. What are the odds of any one of us even being born? The probability of you existing at all comes out to 1 in 102,685,000! Having done the research, Dr. Dina Binazir concludes that the odds of you being alive are basically zero.[1] You are not here by accident. You are here for a purpose; to play your unique part in the cosmic scheme of things and to make a difference that only you can make.

I have counseled hundreds of people from all different backgrounds and have witnessed people questioning their purpose again and again. But remember, you never know what impact you will have on someone else's life or when that opportunity will arise. It may be someone just like you—or only you—who can profoundly touch a person or plant a seed of thought or faith that will grow to impact him or her even more profoundly. The key is just always being you. We are each gifted differently, but we are interconnected in this community of life. Not everyone may appreciate you, but so what? Don't let that be a stumbling block to realizing your purpose. Keep moving forward!

I love the movie *It's a Wonderful Life*. The main character, George Bailey, had his "haters" (e.g., Mr. Potter), but he had no idea the impact he was making on those around him until God showed him with the help of Clarence (a.k.a Angel Second Class). Granted, it's not theologically correct, but the film accurately portrays our existence in this world as crucial to one another.

I think one of my "coincidental" meetings with a stranger named Joe was not so coincidental. Joe is a Holocaust survivor from Poland. He beckoned me over to him after I finished my tour of the Illinois Holocaust Museum and Education Center in Skokie. He was standing in front of a table covered with the book he had authored, yet his eyes told the story, and it was written on his face. My eyes welled up after seeing the pain and hope that he put on display. He placed his hand to his mouth and then to his heart, and in a whispered voice, he said to me, "You understand."

He gave me several grandfatherly hugs and kisses on each cheek. My friend witnessed our interaction and thought Joe and I knew one another because we had acted like family. Workers and volunteers all paused to see our unique connection. It was a very short meeting but one that pierced my heart with sorrow, love, and hope—simultaneously, and I am changed forever. Never underestimate the power of nonverbal communication and the unconditional love of a stranger. Joe may never know how much he affected me, but even that brief, spontaneous connection instilled in me a deeper purpose once again.

During our short meeting, he gave me a piece of himself. He gave me hope.

I've studied the Holocaust for years and have prayed to understand something I did not personally endure. I wanted to know how these amazing people survived physically, mentally, and spiritually. Later, it was revealed that one of my ancestors was twenty-one when he was killed in Auschwitz. I have been to Auschwitz, and years later, am still haunted by it. It's as if I can hear the cries. Yet somehow, their souls transcended the agony of death and triumphed. Deep in my heart I carry their love, passion, pain, sorrow, and hope, and Joe saw that in me. A stranger who looked into my eyes and saw one of the deepest parts of me.

Joe and other survivors taught me that they had to believe they had a purpose for living. Some fought because they desperately wanted to reunite with loved ones. Parents were doing whatever it took to stay alive for their children. Lovers wanted to reunite to spend the rest of their lives together. Some knew that their purpose was to outlast the evil and not let the darkness win. In the Holocaust museums I've toured, there are often areas where you can read the stories of those who were linked and those who miraculously survived. Numbers were tattooed on their arms as the Nazis tried to erase personal identity. They failed. The world would not be denied their stories.

Jim's and my story includes already having our names on our gravestone next to our daughter's and my Grandma Heron's. Since our daughter was the first to be buried in that cemetery, there was a specific standard required of us. We couldn't get the usual child-sized headstone. The monument business told us it was mandatory to get a big one with four names on it and said it was cheaper to include our names at that time. I need not explain how surreal it is to see your name on a tombstone, especially when you're only twenty-four and twenty-three years old. It reminds us that our life will end someday only to begin our eternal journey. But in the meantime . . .

On the headstone there is a line after each of Jim's and my birth dates. Our death dates aren't inscribed yet but we are in the process of living on that little line. As are we all. I saw two guys successfully making that journey: one at the grocery store who greeted people and one at the movie theater who took tickets. They always had genuine smiles. Their attitudes positively impacted mine and, no doubt, others. George Bailey thought he was not making a significant contribution or fulfilling his dreams. However, he found out that his presence was necessary, and it had a domino effect on others. Each person's life does touch another's. We may never know what impact we have on others or why we are in the circumstances we are in, but we need to continue moving on, even if it seems mundane or unfruitful. Our connections with people and experiences are never coincidental.

Recognize that your path may not be the same as others, and it can't be compared. As I took a seat at a table at a wedding, a snooty woman (who shared all her credentials and had a superior-like smirk on her face) asked me what I was doing with my life. She was waiting for me to list my academic degrees and offer my resume.

"I oversee homo sapiens in a Judeo-Christian atmosphere while exposing them to multicultural experiences. I am involved with continuous research to ensure their biological, physiological, psychological, and spiritual needs are met. I encourage the stimulation of the left and right cerebral hemispheres, which are connected by the corpus callosum. In addition, I educate them by using tactile, visual, and auditory activities while creating a continuous loving environment for them." Of course, she seemed rather impressed and had to know what my job title was. I simply answered, "I'm a mom."

Her mouth literally dropped open, and she was speechless at that point.

I usually am not that feisty with people, but I knew she was asking to compare and judge, given her previous comments to others at the table. I love being a mom, and now a grandma. I also have held other "job positions." Here's the deal, though, I am no better or worse than anyone else. I'm just on the path of my journey as we all are.

Again, I think we all just need to be ourselves and take life moment by moment, respecting one another's journey and appreciating everyone's uniqueness! We need to know that we are here for a purpose. When we understand this, it helps to get through the dark times. Even if we feel lost or unsure of our path, we can know that God sees all. He made us and truly desires the best for us.

Psalm 139:13-16 (NIV) explains it well. For you created my inmost being; you knit me together in my mother's womb. I praise you because I am fearfully and wonderfully made; your works are wonderful, I know that full well. My frame was not hidden from you when I was made in the secret place, when I was woven together in the depths of the earth. Your eyes saw my unformed body; all the days ordained for me were written in your book before one of them came to be.

I've also learned that, even though we have our individual journeys and purposes, we all have common ground, even with strangers and those with different backgrounds. In my first book, *The Raindrops on the Windshield Sound Like Popcorn*, I shared what I learned as a therapist in the Illinois Youth Center while counseling male inmates from ages eleven to nineteen. While I would never condone their crimes, I realized that, ultimately, I am no better than them. Given their horrific backgrounds of sex slavery and the abuse that some of these boys endured, I don't know that I would have survived any more successfully than they had. The key to my interaction with them was to impress upon them their worth and purpose because each of the clients assigned to me considered himself worthless and was under suicide watch.

After the first book was written, my friend, Andrea Schmitz, read that chapter and asked if I would speak at the Tribal Prison where she was a therapist. I would end up speaking twice to female inmates there. Both were powerful times of connection. Before I share that experience, I must preface it by saying that some people have asked me how to work with prisoners. I believe that I am no better than them since, like each of us, I am a sinner too. As mentioned, though, that doesn't mean I condone their crimes. When I worked at the Illinois Youth Center as a therapist, I had to read my client's case studies, including their crimes. It was challenging at times because I've counseled victims of similar horrors and have seen the devastation such actions have caused. There have to be consequences for any of our sins.

The amazing thing is God loves us, despite our sins and extends *His* grace to us. God wants us to be successful in our journey to bring Him glory. Many of the youth prisoners had been abused all their lives and were never taught right from wrong. In the case of the incarcerated Native Americans, they deal with an environment most of us can't fathom. That is why I feel it is critical to bring them a message of hope.

Many suffer from addictions to compensate for their depression and anger. I have even had some Native Americans share with me that infants are given alcohol in their bottles to sedate them. Addictions continue from generation to generation until, hopefully, someone breaks the chain one day. Tribal prisons do seek to train and empower inmates to better themselves. I appreciated how the tribal prison referred to inmates as "students" as they learn life skills like parenting, marriage, and self-help. These are lessons that many of us may take for granted.

When I spoke to twelve women prisoners, I did not know their crimes or feel the need to know. They were already suffering the consequences of their actions. I was simply there to tell them that they are loved (which many feel they are not) and that there is hope. In the process, we discussed their purpose, and I heard their beautiful stories reinforcing how each woman is a miracle.

The first time I went to the prison, the women watched me with quizzical looks in their eyes as if to say, "Why is a yuppie white woman here to talk to us?" I opened my talk with that, and they laughed, acknowledging the truth. As I began to share my heart for them, they soon found out that I was there because I cared and that I represented others that were praying for them, a whole team of us. They also found out that I am not a yuppie. I then told them that there were times I didn't want to get out of bed because of the loss of our daughter, suffering after date rape, being in pain due to a chronic illness, etc. Having experienced similar trials, each woman could relate to me on some level. Their own stories reminded me that we *all* have something of value to tell, that we've all endured hardships and have experienced loss. I watched as the barriers broke between us. Because I was raw and real, we connected. It's through our common brokenness that we truly form bonds. It's why strangers feel an instant connection when they experience a trauma or crisis together: no resumes, no pretense—just the real thing.

Using my art therapy background, I had each woman draw a tree. The wonderful thing about art is that it's non-verbal communication. I knew that each tree would be as different as their own names. Those who felt comfortable shared stories of their circumstances, choices, and regrets. I explained how much God loves them and how He had made each woman unique and beautiful. The room fell silent at first, and then sniffles could be heard. Eyes began to water. I then exclaimed, "Thank goodness we are not all alike!" and pointed out that God "does not make junk" (a quote from a bumper sticker). Explaining that they have a purpose caused the corners of their mouths to turn upwards into smiles. Their posture became upright from the downtrodden positions they had just held. Hearing that Jesus came to die in their place to make a new life possible prompted many questions and comments, one being "But I have so much pain inside me." I relayed that after my daughter died, I asked God, at her gravesite, if He knew how painful it was, and He whispered to me, "Yes, I watched My Son die." The heaviness that had been in the room lightened. It was as if a different kind of prison door had opened up.

Then I gave the women one of the most challenging assignments I give people: writing three positive giftings God gave them. This could range from the ability to show love and compassion to cooking to making others laugh. Some began to draw beautiful symbols with brilliant colors on their paper. Some sat there with perplexed looks on their faces. All but one woman finished the project. I then had them share a positive gift they saw in each other. Complimenting another person takes self confidence because bullies belittle others out of insecurity. Narcissistic people are actually deeply insecure. I shared with them that, "We can and should help one another by identifying the positive and being encouraging."

If you know your God-given gifts and realize that no one is perfect, you are more easily able to see the good in others. I also encouraged them not to accept being bullied or abused. Sometimes people need to hear it's okay for them to resist being hurt. They need to forgive those who bully or abuse them (for their own mental health)—but not allow toxic relationships to continue unchecked.

I talked to them about my experience as "Mrs. California International." If God can take a five-foot, two-inch woman with wide hips, brown frizzy hair, and a Chicago accent and make her a California pageant queen, anything is possible! Laughter broke out that also connected us even more. God will use us in ways we can't even imagine if we just allow Him to do so. He uses our very weaknesses for His glory. If we think we have it all together and that it's all about us, we may choose to boast in ourselves, giving ourselves all the credit. When we know our limitations and allow God to work through us, our boasting is in Him.

I explained that I've met many famous people who weren't happy, despite having beauty and money. One can have all kinds of earthly possessions but still not be content. Contentedness comes through understanding that we are loved and that each of us is wonderfully made. As we saw in Psalm 139. This gives us the ability to press on, regardless of our situation!

I shared Revelation 7:17 (AMP) with them. It says there are no more tears in heaven. "For the Lamb who is in the center of the throne will be their Shepherd, and He will guide them to springs of the waters of life, and God will wipe every tear from their eyes [giving them eternal comfort]."

We need to have an eternal perspective. I knew that most of the women might only see Jesus as a historical figure, but I told them about this unique gift of life He gives—temporal and eternal. Having an eternal view has gotten me through some of the most challenging times and helps to keep things in perspective. I go deeper into the eternal perspective in Chapter

4. Hope glistened in their eyes and sparked in their souls as I shared with them that this life is temporary, but they can make the most of their God-given gifts to impact others' lives as well as their own. Their personas began to change and it's as if a kind of confidence came over them to empower them to take steps forward in their lives.

They are already survivors, and they all have a story to tell. In the short time I was with them, I was able to go around the room and talk to each woman individually about what I saw in her through His eyes. As time went on, they all began to open up and share more and more of their stories. They cried as they expressed their pain, grief, and anger. They also laughed. And they seemed to gain the ability to see themselves as uniquely and positively gifted; with an innate ability to survive and thrive!

Each woman drew a symbol representing something personal. Even though a couple drew butterflies, they were each different. Some drew flowers; some drew Native American symbols because of their heritage. Others drew things to represent their children. One woman drew a butterfly with a graduation cap, explaining that she had just earned her GED. She wrote her children's names around that butterfly, hoping to be a positive influence in their lives.

"You will be.", I said.

I explained, once again, that there is hope. We all can change through *His* grace.

Just as I was leaving, one of the women began quoting passages from my first book. I was floored. I don't always know who will read the book or what impact it may have on them. She shared that it was helping her to change her life. She asked for a personal copy as there was only one copy in the prison library. I was more than happy to send her one, but I wondered out loud if anyone else would like one, and they all raised their hands. When I wrote that first book for my children, I had no idea where it would go. I can't take credit for it at all. Only by His grace does it make a difference. One never knows how He can use people!

Those beautiful women presented me with an ice-cream sundae gathering since they learned that I love chocolate. I would be asked to return to that facility again and meet more remarkable women. Like me, like all of us, they were broken in areas looking for hope to heal. Each woman had her own story, symbol, pain, and joys. Each woman's journey touched another's life and ripples onward still.

As I did that morning, I wake up every day and ask God to put me where He wants me. Many people wonder how I end up in the places I do, and now you know. Never limit what God can do! By the way, that meeting was only an hour and a half long but the impact was life-long. We need to recognize every day God gives us twenty-four hours to make a difference. Our purpose may be talking to God in a prayer closet or being an international leader. Each purpose is critical in the big picture.

Taking it deeper, we are made to glorify God. This is the wild thing: God can do anything and everything without us. Yet, He chose to make us, and we get to participate in honoring Him and carrying out His will. He's not even concerned so much with our agendas as He is with us drawing closer to Him. When it is darkest, we surrender fully to Him because there is nothing left but to do so. We lose ourselves only to find the truth that we are nothing without Him.

I learned this from coming close to dying many times. I saw how God could easily give or take life in those times. Somehow, I am still here, despite having congenital medical complications and being diagnosed with multiple disorders. I have shocked several doctors and specialists. God's not done with me yet. He still has me here for a reason. He ordains every breath I breathe. If you are reading this, then He still has work for you to do. I heard somewhere that we don't retire until our life is over. I agree. Let's do it and do it well for our sense of purpose, to better the lives of those around us, and to glorify the God who made us. Again, check that heart of yours. Is it beating? Then you still are here for a purpose.

I often reflect on something my husband wrote after our first daughter died. It sums up our purpose here on earth.

Meanwhile, the adventure continues for those of us in the human condition. We said goodbye to one so innocent who very briefly made an appearance in this world, taught us many things, and went home. Now we must continue with the lessons learned. Our purpose is to journey through this life working unto the Lord, praying without ceasing, rejoicing always, giving thanks, and most importantly, spreading the gospel.

Endnotes

1 Dina Spector, "The Odds of You Being Alive Are Incredibly Small," March 12, 2013, https://www.businessinsider.com.au/infographic-the-odds-of-being-alive-2012-6.

CHAPTER 2

COMMUNITY & FELLOWSHIP

I couldn't figure out which chapter to review as I edited this book the other night. I kept going back to the one on "Community." I need not elaborate on how this is a hot topic with the COVID-19 pandemic and how our world has flipped upside down. Little did I know that God was prompting me to look at it because the concept of community would be critical the next day.

On Tuesday morning, I began receiving many calls and messages simultaneously. Something was wrong. I hesitated a moment because, as with last year, there's been an overload of negative events. Never would I have guessed that it would be the devastating news that a close friend who was a "brother from another mother" had unexpectedly passed away. Disbelief, deep sorrow, and pain gripped my heart. He, along with others and myself, had just recently video chatted. We had all laughed until our cheeks hurt. We also shared how meaningful our friendships were to each other over the years.

So, "Why, God?!" Our friend has an amazing wife and daughters. They had just celebrated his birthday together the day before.

Those of us who knew him offered one another comfort. We grieved with one another, understanding that it's important to have each other's backs.

I began to look through photos with my friend in them. His smile was contagious. He was the kind of extroverted person who just lit up a room and brought joy into people's lives. A picture of the two of us caught my attention. There, in the background, was the word "COMMUNITY" on the wall. I knew in an instant that this was not coincidental. That's why God had me work on that very chapter the night before. I realized that there was so much beauty in the wake of this deep pain. A deep community came together to walk through this trial together, to help the family and one another. I knew then that I was supposed to go back and reread what God had shown me to write. Whether you're an introvert, an extrovert, or somewhere in-between, we *all* need community right now. You may be as charismatic as my friend, or you may be like one of those quiet pastors who visited Nelson Mandela in prison and were just as crucial as he was in the process of fighting apartheid. Everyone plays their part in the community, and again, we need one another. I hope the following story encourages you.

I felt isolated and frightened after losing my friend, but then something amazing happened. Jim and I had been on a trip to New York. I had to fly out of Newark Airport while Jim had to drive to Pennsylvania for business. He didn't want to leave me, but I assured him that I would be all right and didn't want him stuck in the major storm heading our way. Having already called the airlines ahead of my arrival to make a "special assistance request" for a wheelchair, I was sure I'd be fine.

To my surprise, the personnel gave me no help other than having someone wheel me into a corner by the ticketing agent's counter. He left me sitting in a broken-down airport wheelchair as he went to find my "lost" personal wheelchair. The assistant never returned. Physically, I had been doing pretty well with only minor symptoms that week, but the major storm front was coming through our area. As the barometric pressure dropped, my body reacted. I felt the tingling in my head and the sensation of ants crawling down my spine. I knew my congenital situation was being triggered.

The seizure began, the left side of my face drew tight, and I couldn't speak. My hands refused to budge the white childproof cap of the medication bottle. Through tears, I realized that three people were coming my way. As they came near and into focus, I realized that three amazing New Jersey police officers had seen the trouble I was in and were there to help me. They made sure I had what I needed and then angrily addressed the airline personnel for not assisting me. Finally, when I did make it through security and onto the airplane, I sat back with a sigh and waited for takeoff. For three hours, we stayed on the runway due to the raging storm.

By then, I had missed my connecting flight from Phoenix to California, so I contacted Jim. He called the airlines and then made hotel arrangements for me in Phoenix with a hotel that had a shuttle service. After three hours, we were brought back to the terminal and allowed to deplane temporarily. I didn't know how to do it since they wanted us to take our luggage. I was still so weak, and my left side was somewhat paralyzed. However, I was sitting next to Tony and Beth, a very sweet Italian couple.

They had shown me photos of their family and told me of the wonderful meals they cook together. Tony and Beth overheard the flight attendant talking with me and decided to take me under their wing. Tony helped with my carry-ons, and they graciously treated me to dinner in the terminal. Here were two strangers who showed me kindness and helped me when I couldn't help myself. When we were able to get back on the airplane, the rain had stopped and there was a full rainbow in the sky. I don't think it was coincidental. As it turns out, it wasn't.

When I got to Phoenix, I said goodbye to my new friends on the plane and told them that I should be receiving assistance from the airline. My wheelchair was still missing. So, being the last person off the plane, I had to walk up the jet bridge dragging my left leg as well as my carry-ons. I knew I was about to miss the last shuttle to the hotel. I literally had fifteen minutes left before I'd have to find other transportation.

Again, I was doing my best to be brave and thanking God for Tony and Beth, who had just helped me. I sent up another prayer. In answer, a man came up and asked if he could help me. We found my wheelchair folded up by the gate agents' station and took off at a half-run, the front wheel of the chair shaking like it was on a shopping cart. He got me onto the shuttle in time for which I was so grateful. It was midnight as I arrived at the hotel, thankful that Jim had found a place for me to stay. I felt a sense of peace. Only a handful of people had known what was happening and it made such a difference knowing that they were praying for me. After another delay the next morning, I finally made it home.

After that experience, I was adopted! Let me explain. There are kind hearts everywhere and good can come out of even the most challenging trials. The next day, Beth called to check if I made it home okay and was choked up on the phone. She shared how Tony's 90-plus-year-old mom heard the story and had started praying for me. Having never met me, she said she needed to talk to me on the phone. I won't go into what she said (it blew me away), but she ended by stating that she was adopting me as her granddaughter and would continue to pray for me daily. I cried tears of joy.

I had just been thinking of how much I missed my grandparents and how they would tell me they would pray for me, including my grandma, who went to heaven earlier that year. Needless to say, Josephine, my new grandma, and I connected instantly. She sent a letter and a drawing she made for me with a rainbow. I never tire of being in awe of how strangers can affect your life. I now have a Grandma Jo! A few years later, Jim and I returned to New Jersey, where Jim met Tony and Beth! Sadly, since the writing of this book, Grandma Jo passed away. I am so glad I will get to see her someday in heaven.

That is just one example of how strangers can become part of your community, friends, and even "family." As I write this, though, we've had two years of pandemic. We have been under lockdown, walking around with masks, and staying six feet apart. We've had limited socialization. Children, teens, and college students have been doing school by video. Businesses have closed; social events have been canceled. There have been rallies and riots. I could go on and on, but if there was ever a time when we needed to socialize, this is definitely one of those times. In one way, technology has been an enormous blessing. However, social media has done us a great deal of harm as well.

More than ever, our world is connected through technology. But we are more lonely than ever because as much as social media has its benefits, it has also contributed to increased depression and isolation. We need face-to-face, in-person connection since most communication is nonverbal. The Bible talks about community as being crucial: "Rejoice with those who rejoice; mourn with those who mourn" (Romans 12:15 NIV),

Numerous studies show that infants fail to thrive unless they have physical touch. Hugs and kisses have been proven to increase endorphins and serotonin levels, which help the brain, heart, and immune system. You can watch videos of the moment a child or adult sees or hears for the first time that show the value of connection. No, this is not necessary for bonding, but it does show the significance of communication. My dear friend and daughter-in-law's mom says it's better to communicate in 3D. She lives in Germany, and therefore we have a long-distance relationship. We can be thankful for technology to connect us. Yet, there is nothing like being in person.

Also, it's interesting to note that cultures that promote community are so much more content than those that don't. I live in the United States and envy those places that have town squares where people can go to connect. Before the pandemic, we seemed so busy that there was not enough time for social gatherings. I don't think we will ever take time with others for granted after this time in history. Wherever I've lived, I have been determined to bring people together. The healing that happens naturally when people are united is wonderful! I love seeing people laughing and enjoying each other's company. In addition to this, though, I do understand the need to be alone.

My personality type is both introvert and extrovert. So, I need that downtime, too, sometimes.

Even though you may be a *pure* introvert or a *pure* extrovert, there are times when God wants you to do things that would be counter to your natural tendency. He may wish the extrovert to spend some time alone with Him to be filled. He may want the introvert to trust and rely on others for support because when we are going through something challenging, we need others. We were made for fellowship. Please do not walk this journey of life alone.

We often feel that we are the only ones enduring such pain, that no one else would understand, or that we don't want to be a bother. I have been observing more and more that true community—genuine fellowship—occurs when people are broken and come together. Moses of Exodus was commanded to hold up his arms towards heaven.

> As long as Moses held up his hands, the Israelites were winning, but whenever he lowered his hands, the Amalekites were winning. When Moses' hands grew tired, they took a stone and put it under him and he sat on it. Aaron and Hur held his hands up—one on one side, one on the other—so that his hands remained steady till sunset. (Exodus 17:11-12 NIV)

When he grew tired, his brother and friend held up his arms. He did not do it alone. Why we insist on going through things by ourselves so often puzzles me. Family and friends can pray for us when we feel like we can't. The accountability, encouragement, and support of others are critical. Tony carried my luggage when I couldn't do it myself.

Not only can others help us, but we can help them. Someone once asked me if I love to help others.

"Yes, definitely!"

"Then why don't you allow others the same pleasure of helping you?"

Ouch! So true! It's scary to let others into our world when things are complex and less than perfect. Yet, it is at these times when we need help the most.

There is another side to community. Sometimes we are supposed to be alone because God is jealous and wants us to rely entirely on Him. Jesus was alone in the desert. "Jesus, full of the Holy Spirit, left the Jordan and was led by the Spirit into the wilderness, where for forty days he was tempted by the devil. He ate nothing during those days, and at the end of them he was hungry." (Luke 4:1-2 NIV).

It's not easy to be alone, though. As mentioned at the beginning of this chapter, there have been times when I've felt isolated even if I had others around me because of the trials

I was enduring. I have been on the floor face down before God, crying out to Him. He seems distant at those times but remember, you are never alone because the One who created you will never leave you! "God is our refuge and strength, an ever-present help in trouble. Therefore we will not fear, though the earth give way and the mountains fall into the heart of the sea," (Psalm 46:1-2 NIV).

Jesus was abandoned and alone in Gethsemane; He endured intense pain in obedience to His father and also because of His indescribable love for us. He allows you to identify with some of that pain to gain a deeper understanding of just how much He cares for you.

How can you discern between reaching out or being alone with Him? I wish I had an easy answer for that, but I do think there are times you may feel it necessary to listen carefully to Him. Being silent before Him to hear His still, small voice can be challenging but worth it. At other times, you may need to see God work through others. Corrie ten Boom (a survivor of Ravensbrück Concentration Camp) stated, "There is no pit so deep that God's love is not deeper still."[1] He *is* our hope, strength, and joy. God is love! He loves you and is there for you. He also works through those he has prepared excellent work to do. That good work may be directed toward you!

He is the rainbow in the dark.

Endnotes

1   Kaylena Radcliff, "A war story: There is no pit so deep God's love is not deeper still," June 28, 2017, https://www.christiantoday.com/article/a-war-story-there-is-no-pit-so-deep-gods-love-is-not-deeper-still/110251.htm.

CHAPTER 3

UNANSWERED PRAYERS

I've been asked about healing and if it matters how much or how well you pray. Nope! Does prayer help us? Yep! Nick Vujicic, born without limbs, hasn't acquired arms and legs and has positively impacted thousands of lives. Because of what Nick's endured and his hope in God, he has touched the hearts of multitudes worldwide. Prayer is about intimacy and communication with a loving Father. If you believe that Jesus loves and died for you, going to heaven is amazing!

We hate death because of the mourning we go through. Yet, there is no pain or tears for those we love who get promoted— the ultimate healing. Why did our first daughter, Elizabeth, go to heaven? And why am I still here (my medical doctors will tell you it's a miracle, but I, without any reservation, would have given my life for hers)? I don't have the answers, but I know God sees the bigger picture. I've learned to praise Him in the storms, and of course, gotta love those rainbows.

What about other unanswered prayers? The top theologians can't give complete answers as to why our prayers don't always get answered. Yet, we know God does hear every prayer. Here is a key verse: "This is the confidence we have in approaching God: that if we ask anything according to his will, he hears us" (1 John 5:14 NIV).

I am a nerd at heart and study quantum physics. Nope, I will not attempt an explanation as there are many books on it, and I don't feel I would do an adequate job. However, the more I study molecules, mathematical sequences in nature (e.g., fractal geometry), physiology of the brain, or our genetic makeup, the more I am convinced that God is sovereign. God created this beautiful universe for us, but things changed with the fall of Adam and Eve. Illness, broken relations, and other problems entered God's creation. In addition, God doesn't want us to be puppets, so we have free will (a.k.a. permissive will). His will is perfect, and He wants us to have ours aligned with His as He knows what's best for us. So, we are directed to pray:

> Our Father, Who art in heaven
> Hallowed be Thy Name;
> Thy kingdom come,
> Thy will be done
> on earth as it is in heaven. (Matthew 6:9-10 KJV)

What if we don't know how to pray for something? "In the same way, the Spirit helps us in our weakness. We do not know what we ought to pray for, but the Spirit himself intercedes for us through wordless groans" (Romans 8:26 NIV). I am so thankful for this verse. We are imperfect people who need a perfect God. This verse exemplifies His love again in that even when we are unsure how to pray, He still has us covered.

Unanswered prayers usually mean that disappointment and even suffering may be involved. What does God say about suffering?

Therefore, since we have been justified through faith, we have peace with God through our Lord Jesus Christ, through whom we have gained access by faith into this grace in which we now stand. And we boast in the hope of the glory of God. Not only so, but we also glory in our sufferings, because we know that suffering produces perseverance; perseverance, character; and character, hope. And hope does not put us to shame, because God's love has been poured out into our hearts through the Holy Spirit, who has been given to us. (Romans 5:1-5 NIV)

And another good verse: "And after you have suffered a little while, the God of all grace, who has called you to His eternal glory in Christ, will himself restore, confirm, strengthen, and establish you" (1 Peter 5:10 ESV).

I get that trusting God is sometimes not easy when a person experiences broken dreams, toxic people, unfulfilled expectations, or unanswered prayers. We will face mountains like this. Either God will move the mountain, help us climb over it, or direct us the long way around it. And when we are tired or feel weak, He will carry us.

Also, it's hard to see when fires burn things down in nature, but I've witnessed new life pop up in what looks like apocalyptic scenes. Sometimes, it doesn't take too long, and other times, it takes years, but restoration happens. As Isaiah 61:3 discusses, "Beauty for ashes." There were a lot of "mountains" and fires in 2020 and 2021, but God did not leave us. If we trust Him, He will continue not just to guide or carry us but provide hope for the future. Here are two passages that exemplify that:

> The Spirit of the Sovereign Lord is on me,
> because the Lord has anointed me
> to proclaim good news to the poor.
> He has sent me to bind up the brokenhearted,
> to proclaim freedom for the captives
> and release from darkness for the prisoners,
> to proclaim the year of the Lord's favor
> and the day of vengeance of our God,
> to comfort all who mourn,
> and provide for those who grieve in Zion—
> to bestow on them a crown of beauty
> instead of ashes,
> the oil of joy

instead of mourning,

and a garment of praise

instead of a spirit of despair.

They will be called oaks of righteousness,

a planting of the Lord

for the display of his splendor. (Isaiah 61:1-3 NIV)

You turned my wailing into dancing;

you removed my sackcloth and clothed me with joy,

that my heart may sing your praises and not be silent.

Lord my God, I will praise you forever. (Psalm 30:11-12 NIV)

I felt it important to include my husband's thoughts on unanswered prayers. In the book *The Raindrops on the Windshield Sound Like Popcorn*, I wrote about our experience with our daughter dying a slow death. If you read it, you understand my perspective of the situation. During our experience and afterward, I had many people I could talk with who shared similar experiences. However, Jim noticed that fathers of children in the PICU often would go to the bar.

I pray for men to be able to sit at the elder's gates (Proverbs 31:23 NIV) and have the opportunity to talk about the complicated issues we all face. Our brains all process things like unanswered prayers differently. Research from Goldman found that "brain-imaging studies indicate that these differences extend well beyond the strictly reproductive domain, Cahill says. Adjusted for total brain size (men's are bigger), a woman's hippocampus, critical to learning and memorization, is larger than a man's and works differently. Conversely, a man's amygdala, associated with the experiencing of emotions and the recollection of such experiences, is bigger than a woman's."[1]

"Unanswered" Prayers by Jim

As I drove my VW Bug those forty-six miles on Chicago freeways each of those winter nights to Christ Hospital, I thought about many things. I thought about being married for a year and a half, about having just graduated from chiropractic college two months before. I thought about the almost-but-not-quite job in Hawaii as snowplows sprayed frozen slush on the side of my car. Mostly, I thought about my newborn daughter lying in her NICU crib and my wife by her side. I hadn't spent much time inside a hospital since the riding lawnmower incident when I was eight years old that took the outside half of my left heel. Those were the days before safety switches in the seat that turned the mower off in case of an unexpected ejection. Those were also the days before effective methods of repairing a severed Achilles tendon. Thankfully, mine was left intact by the narrowest of margins. Lucky, right?

A skin graft and a foot and leg cast were misapplied and then removed a month later, leaving my left foot crooked. The resultant waddling walk earned me the nickname "Penguin" from my Little League team and my classmates at school. I like penguins, but I did everything to correct that issue, including praying. Having grown up in a Christian home and in a church that was very much a community of believers, we prayed. Silently, out-loud, liturgically, and conversationally. With humble reverence and with bold authority, formulas, and freeform; if there was a way to pray, I heard it.

My dad was the head elder at the church, and the twelve elders were occasionally summoned to hospitals to pray for and anoint the sick with oil like the Bible says to do and, sometimes, miracles happened. Not just that people recovered when they probably would have anyway, but real, medical/science-defying events that could not be explained with any other word than "miracle." And we celebrated and talked about those events.

So, when Wednesday nights rolled around, we went to "Prayer and Praise" or healing services that were telecast on the big screen. I was eight years old and went forward—every time—to receive my healing. And every time, as I recall, a somewhat skeptical pastor or lay leader humored me and prayed for my foot to be healed. I don't remember when I resigned myself to the fact that God wasn't going to heal my foot. It was not without disappointment or wondering why I was stuck with a grotesque scar, but experience is truth, so I accepted it eventually. Or is it?

Fast forward seventeen years to the winter of 1990-91 when our one-month-old daughter, Elizabeth, desperately needed a miracle. I knew they could happen and, naturally, if God could perform miracles and didn't, I wanted (and at times demanded) to know why. Either He was choosing (again?) to withhold the miracle that was totally within His ability to grant, or something was preventing Him from granting the miracle. Or maybe both were true. Or maybe neither.

Can we really know how God operates? "Then the LORD answered Job out of a whirlwind and said 'Who is this that darkens counsel by words without knowledge? Now gird up your loins like a man, and I will ask you, and you will instruct me! Where were you when I laid the foundation of the earth? Tell me, if you have understanding . . .'" You know the rest.

(Btw, my intention in quoting the first verse or so of the passage (in this case, Job 38 AMPC) is the same as when it was done in biblical times. Quoting the beginning portion of a passage prompted the audience to remember the full text and context of that passage or to review it for themselves i.e. Jesus quoting the beginning of Psalm 22 from the cross. You have to look at the whole of Psalm 22 to understand what Jesus was referencing there.)

Anyway, we are not left in total ignorance. God The Holy Spirit does give us insight and understanding if only to "see through a glass darkly" for now. Frustrating? Yes. Easy for us to misinterpret things and defend differences of opinion?

Yes. With opportunities to study and show yourself approved to God, a worker who does not need to be ashamed, rightly dividing the word of truth (2 Timothy 2:15)? Absolutely!

There are so many knowledgeable people in the Christian community whose studying and research can become a springboard for our own. "Rightly dividing the word of truth" does not mean jumping on someone's bandwagon just because others have or because it's easier than thinking through an issue or concept yourself and testing your conclusions in light of God's Word. So, keep thinking, study both sides of an issue, and pray for insight from God, the Holy Spirit, before drawing a conclusion. Even then, we've got to be open to further insight as the process continues.

I've heard it said that a conclusion is often the point at which someone gets tired of thinking. By the way, I do believe this to be the case when people tell me that their doctor's conclusion was that they would just have to "learn to live with it." Growing in knowledge, wisdom, understanding, and discernment is a process that can be highly enjoyable and frustrating at the same time. At the limit of our current location in that process is where faith sustains us.

My eight-year-old self was more highly dependent on faith as a substitute for knowable things than I am now. Still, even now, the featherweight of my knowledge, wisdom, understanding, and discernment is incomparable to my lack of the same. When I was a child, I had the faith of a child. Was it not enough faith to prompt a healing? Well, that is a topic for another day, I think.

So, where am I on my journey now? My personality lends itself to a more intellectual approach to God. I know what I know, and I know there's plenty that I don't know. I believe certain things based on this and what my experiences have taught me. Forty-six years ago, I believed in God without knowing much. My misunderstanding about God at the time was that He failed, for whatever reason, to heal my foot.

In 1974, doctors told my parents I would have multiple subsequent surgeries. Skin graft technology was not very advanced at the time, and my graft would require replacement as I grew into adulthood. The miracle is that I've never needed a follow-up surgery. Not one. While I was praying for healing at those Wednesday night services, my heel did not morph back to normal as I had hoped, but God was answering my prayers. He didn't take away the constant reminder of that experience. And whatever "suffering" it caused, it produced in me perseverance, character, and hope, as the Bible says. I eventually learned to sleep on my back with the covers tucked under my heels and my left foot turned inward in a make-shift splint for hours every night, reducing the waddle. Though, not before that uneven gait affected my back enough to contribute to scoliosis.

Even though I didn't play much Little League after 1974, I did go on to participate in track and field in junior high school, five years of wrestling, and four years of football. By the time I finished high school, my scoliosis had been corrected from nineteen to 1.75 degrees with chiropractic care and the exercise of sports. This, in turn, put me on my career path. "And we know that God causes all things to work together for good to those who love God, to those who are called according to His purpose" (Romans 8:28 NASB).

But how could the death of our child be "for the good"? We are still walking that out. On April 1, 1991, we got the call from the Christ Hospital NICU nurses who had become our friends, telling us that Elizabeth was fading and to come quickly. In a time before social media, literally hundreds, if not thousands, of people were praying for a miraculous recovery. That morning, Elizabeth died in Colleen's arms with me by their side. Again, prayer had failed us all.

Some people accused Colleen and me of having inadequate faith. I believe that in some circumstances, God makes the outcome dependent on our participation. I don't believe that was the case in this situation. The miracle was that God gave both Colleen and me, together, insight into this inevitable outcome two weeks before it happened. At that shared moment, we came into complete alignment with God's plan for Elizabeth's short life. It was by no means easy after that, and we did grieve hard, but we also had peace. We didn't blame God and weren't mad at Him because Elizabeth touched so many other peoples' lives in the four and a half months that God had allotted for her life. We still hear stories about it and are grateful to have been part of it.

Several years after Elizabeth's death, I wondered about the purpose and power of prayer. Is it solely to align us with God's will so we can roll with it, "good or bad," and accept our place in it? Can prayer really change things? Does it depend on a quantity or quality of faith or a certain level of faithfulness? Is God "limited" in His ability to intervene by His very nature, which is Love? Does that last sentence sound logically inconsistent? Are prayers cumulative before they "work"? Is it wrong or selfish to pray for personal needs? Does God have more important issues to deal with?

The Bible tells us that God requires three things of us: to pray constantly, to rejoice, and to give thanks in everything. So, there must be something to prayer, and God must be expecting to hear from us. You've probably asked similar questions to the ones I've asked. There are answers to be found that make sense and don't violate Scripture. Keep searching.

"It is the glory of God to conceal a matter; to search out a matter is the glory of kings" (Proverbs 25:2 NIV).

Endnotes

1   Bruce Goldman, "Two minds: The cognitive differences between men and women," 2017, https://stanmed.stanford.edu/2017spring/how-mens-and-womens-brains-are-different.html.

CHAPTER 4

ETERNAL PERSPECTIVE

I have my funeral planned. I won't share all the details, but it does include a chocolate festival and dancing after the service. I figured if they party at funerals in New Orleans, why can't I have that too? Which reminds me, note to self: Add bagpipes for a touch of Irish (I have some Scottish in me too, and while I am at it, there should be some Greek and Jewish dancing.)

Also, I would love to be like Tom Sawyer and attend my funeral, as I hope it's a joyful celebration. No, I am not being morbid, nor do I have a death wish, as I would have been gone long ago since I've come close to dying so many times. I just like having my "ducks in a row." I also know how painful it can be to plan a funeral, having planned our daughter's, my Grandma Heron's, and my dad's. I want to help limit the stress for my family and friends after I "go up to the Spirit in the sky." Just recently, I updated some of the funeral details with Jim. Inevitably, it will happen someday, but like several of my family and friends have said, I will probably be dancing into my nineties or hundreds.

I am not afraid to die because heaven will be amazing! No . . . more than amazing . . . indescribable! Seeing Jesus face-to-face and being embraced by Him with no more tears or pain is totally beyond my finite comprehension.

In my first book, I share that two weeks before our daughter entered heaven, Jim and I had an experience (no drugs or alcohol were used) in which we felt a peace beyond understanding. We believe God gave us a glimpse of where Elizabeth was going. It helped us get through the next two weeks of her life, which was full of pain as we watched her slowly slip away. Oh, we fought in prayer with everything in us for her to be healed. When she transitioned to heaven, we felt the deepest pain and the strangest peace. We knew she wouldn't have to experience any more trials. We also have learned to embrace life! We live boldly! Perhaps that is why I can share this with you. This is not our final home but just the steppingstone before it. "Holy, Holy, Holy, is the Lord God Almighty, who was, and is, and is to come!" (Revelation 4:8 NIV). When I die, I will experience a sweet homecoming with my Savior, daughter, and other loved ones.

Keeping an eternal perspective is important. This life is temporary. As children of God, we have the promise of eternity in heaven. "And God shall wipe away all tears from their eyes; and there shall be no more death, neither sorrow, nor crying, neither shall there be any more pain: for the former things are passed away" (Revelation 21:4 KJV). This is such a challenging concept at times. We are used to the "here and now." We want smooth sailing and immediate gratification. Yet, there is a bigger picture.

There is *nothing* wrong with celebrating the good moments in life! However, posts on social media often alter our perception of reality. *No* person or family is perfect. All people and families deal with trials. It could be a loss due to death or divorce, an illness, or financial struggles. There can be relational conflict. Due to the pandemic and all, the use of social media has skyrocketed.

Being a therapist, I am well aware that many people have been discouraged by social media, and several suffer from depression, especially during the holidays. I believe one of the reasons is what I call the "Christmas Card Syndrome." Around the holidays, we send photos and newsletters or post pictures to social media that primarily show all the positive things in our lives . . . *and we should*! There is *nothing* wrong with celebrating the good moments in life! However, as mentioned above, no person or family is perfect.

In November 1990, our first child was born. I was so excited about her first Thanksgiving, Christmas, New Year, Valentine's Day, St. Patrick's Day, and Easter. Yet, we spent each of these holidays in the Pediatric Intensive Care Unit. Our Thanksgiving meal that year was cafeteria food. We made the best of it, but it was still not what the movies or commercials portrayed. It was not what I thought our Christmas photo would look like. You never know what adventures life will bring to you, including during the holidays. So, how should we deal with "Christmas Card Syndrome" or just the negative sides of social media?"

1) COUNT YOUR BLESSINGS

I will give thanks to you, LORD, with all my heart;
I will tell of all your wonderful deeds. (Psalm 9:1 NIV)

Did you know that even Norman Rockwell dealt with depression?[1] He still found positive things to paint, despite his emotions. This is not always easy to do, but take a moment, grab a pen and paper, and start writing down the blessings in your life. No matter how tough life gets, you can always be thankful for something. I've experienced very tough times, hoping the earth would swallow me up or have prayed, "Beam me up to heaven now, please!" Then I take a deep breath, pray, grab some chocolate, look around, and count my blessings.

2) REMEMBER, YOU ARE WORTH IT!

For the gifts and the calling of God are irrevocable [for He does not withdraw what He has given, nor does He change His mind about those to whom He gives His grace or to whom He sends His call]. (Romans 11:29 AMP)

I think many people feel isolated during the holidays. They may not want to celebrate by putting up decorations and all. Remember George again in *It's a Wonderful Life*. He felt that way; he felt overwhelmed and wanted to give up. He thought life had cheated him. However, he found out his life was worth it. So is yours! I truly believe God doesn't make mistakes. You can make a difference and already have. You may never know how much you mean in someone else's life. So you've made mistakes? We all have! If we were perfect, we wouldn't need God!

3) LAUGH

A happy heart is good medicine and a joyful mind causes healing, But a broken spirit dries up the bones. (Proverbs 17:22 AMP)

There's nothing like laughing until your cheeks and stomach hurt. Laughter is scientifically proven to increase serotonin and endorphin levels. It burns calories and can work your core. It's known to be contagious and something you actually want to catch. It builds the immune system. Find family and friends to laugh with, or a video or movie. Just go for it! We need more laughter in this world.

4) SERVE OR GIVE

Each of you should use whatever gift you have received to serve others, as faithful stewards of God's grace in its various forms. (1 Peter 4:10 NIV)

Thinking of ways to bless others and then following through is one of the best ways to overcome the blues. Do it without any expectations other than to encourage someone else. You can give a gift. If you are financially strapped, dollar stores have some of the coolest things if you look. Or make a homemade gift. It's not about the money but the thought.

You can make a meal or even help clean or organize if someone has a tough time doing that. Have a listening ear. Our time and presence are great ways to give. There are countless ways, but it sends a ripple effect. Paying it forward is real and makes the world a better place.

5) KEEP IT SIMPLE

"Be still, and know that I am God; I will be exalted among the nations, I will be exalted in the earth." (Psalm 46:10 NIV)

The less you own, the less you're responsible for, the less you have to clean, and the less money you spend. When we moved across the country, we had to get rid of a house full of stuff. Yes, it was hard because of attached memories, but we did keep some items. At the same time, it was so freeing. I am doing an early spring cleaning right now. You learn you don't need a lot to live on. Decluttering physically can help declutter the mind.

Don't put up decorations during the holidays if it's too stressful. It's OK if it's too overwhelming; the agony is not worth it. When we were relocating to Iowa, Jim needed to move before us because of work. I had twenty-four-hour "morning sickness" and was raising three little ones. The most I could do was put up socks (our stockings were packed) and make paper snowflakes. We ate bologna sandwiches for Christmas. It worked. Try to keep it simple. I would suggest doing something you enjoy during the holidays. Your mood may change while engaging in the activity.

And since I coined the term "Christmas Card Syndrome," I want to encourage you to remember that a child was born for you. A loving Father was willing to sacrifice His Son. He sent him to earth because He loves *you* that much! Only by God's grace have I been able to send "Merry" Christmas photo cards and newsletters or post pictures on social media. I don't take any of these moments for granted. I accept the good times when they come and celebrate. I enjoy looking at others' photos, knowing that they too can experience miracles in their lives. I understand that things are not always perfect for them and am so thankful when they sense God's grace and peace.

6) FOCUS ON GOD'S GRACE

"My grace is sufficient for you [My lovingkindness and My mercy are more than enough—always available—regardless of the situation]; for [My] power is being perfected [and is completed and shows itself most effectively] in [your] weakness." (2 Corinthians 12:9 AMP)

Let's take it even deeper. I recall going through very difficult trials, such as watching my daughter die or having to let go of a foster child we were in the process of adopting or identifying my grandma's body after a fatal car accident. These trials tested my faith at first. They shook me to my core, and I wondered why God would allow such trials. Then, I recall the Christians I read about who worshiped in church with one hand on their throat, signifying that they were willing to die for their faith, and the other hand raised and praising God. Then, a terrorist came into their church and killed most of them. Why would God allow that? Why, especially, if they were in the middle of worshiping Him? God gently spoke to me, saying that He did protect them. The enemy could not touch their souls. They had eternal life. "Even though I walk through the darkest valley, I will fear no evil, for you are with me; your rod and your staff, they comfort me" (Psalm 23:4 NIV).

Sometimes, we are stripped of worldly things to focus on the eternal. The light shines brighter in the dark. It's challenging to go through trials. But when we understand that this life is temporary, we can take comfort in knowing that the trials will pass. I have learned from others and my own experiences that if God were to take everything away, we would still have the most critical thing: His love.

Job understood this. God allowed Satan to take away his children, finances, health, etc. Of course, Job was downhearted and perplexed, but he could get to that place where he knew that God made him and saw all. Job came to understand that if all is taken away, God remains. Job exclaimed, "I know that my redeemer lives, and that in the end he will stand on the earth. And after my skin has been destroyed, yet in my flesh, I will see God" (Job 19:25-26 NIV).

Some dear friends of ours lost much. They lived in a country where Christians were being imprisoned and killed. They were running a little late to their church service, which was held in a home (an underground church). As they came into view of the house, they saw that their family and friends were being arrested and dragged away. They escaped to another country where they didn't know anyone or the language. They still do not know what has happened to many of their loved ones, and the pain they endure goes deep. Despite this, they purposely strive to move forward and keep the eternal perspective in mind.

During the Cambodian Holocaust, a pastor friend was severely persecuted. He was placed in a prison cell so small he needed to crouch. He heard God tell him to eat nothing. You see, his persecutors thought he was some political enemy or spy because he had a following of people. They wanted him to live so he could be interrogated. Starving himself was unacceptable. So, he ended up in a hospital where he met a Christian doctor from America. This man told him he would meet him outside that night. This idea seemed impossible as guards were stationed all over the hospital. Yet, there was a massive storm, and the electricity went out. My friend escaped the hospital, and he crawled under a gate to his freedom, where the doctor was waiting with a car.

My friend could have given up. He had already witnessed loved ones being beaten and killed. Because he believed in Jesus as his Savior, he knew he had the promise of eternal life. Also, he knew that this wasn't his time to die unless God chose for his life to end. He embraced the thought that his trial was all for the moment and would pass sooner or later. More incredible things were sure to come. "For momentary, light affliction is producing for us an eternal weight of glory far beyond all comparison, while we look not at the things which are seen, but at the things which are not seen; for the things which are seen are temporal, but the things which are not seen are eternal" (2 Corinthians 4:17-18 NASB).

Years afterward, this pastor continues to evangelize and encourage thousands. In his brokenness, he identified more with Jesus. By God's grace, he now confidently talks about overcoming trials and is fulfilling his purpose of sharing God's faithfulness and His promise of eternal life.

While I can't fathom what my friends have endured, I, too, have lost much in my life (children and other loved ones, health, finances, etc.). Admittedly, I am not always joyful during these times and, as I've said, have even found myself face down on a floor, crying out to God to take away the pain. Sometimes, I have been so frustrated that I asked God why He would take away people and things if He were a loving Father. Then, I am reminded of Jesus' time in Gethsemane. He was about to face a trial that we could never fully comprehend. He cried, "Now My soul is troubled and distressed, and what shall I say? Father, save Me from this hour [of trial and agony]? But it was for this very purpose that I have come to this hour [that I might undergo it]" (John 12:27 AMPC).

Hebrews 4:15-16 (NIV) gives me great comfort: "For we do not have a high priest who is unable to empathize with our weaknesses, but we have one who has been tempted in every way, just as we are—yet he did not sin. Let us then approach

God's throne of grace with confidence, so that we may receive mercy and find grace to help us in our time of need." He endured the deepest pain because of His love for us. We can identify with His suffering through our trials and understand His love even more. Because of this great love, we can live a life of purpose here and have hope to live forever with Him in heaven.

Eternal Perspective

Endnotes

1 "Behind Rockwell's Idyllic America, There Were a Lot of Therapy Bills," November 1, 2013, https://www.npr.org/2013/11/01/240538151/behind-rockwells-idyllic-america-there-were-a-lot-of-therapy-bills.

CHAPTER 5

DON'T GIVE UP! NAVY SEAL KIND OF THINKING

Most mornings when I wake up now, my body feels like it's attacking itself. My brain tells my legs to swing off the side of the bed, but the delay in actually doing it is concerning. I have to be determined to set foot on the floor. Some days, it's relatively easy, while others, my body does not want to cooperate. Some days, I experience pain, weakness, imbalance, or shaking so violently that it's not even feasible to attempt to stand. It takes prayer and repeating scriptures to overcome it all, and eventually, I manage to get up.

I know I am not alone in this, and so many struggle to get out of bed. It's not just because of their physical health but for other reasons too. It's a harsh world out there, and it doesn't seem to be getting any easier. My friend Todd Green was walking by a baseball field his son was playing on when a branch fell directly on his head, resulting in severe spinal trauma that left him paralyzed from the chest down. Here's what he wrote:

What will I push myself to accomplish today in therapy? I will push myself to continue on this road to recovery that I started seven months ago. Pain, happiness, and depression are things I deal with on any given day. For some time, I struggled with what cards I had been dealt. I spent a month lying in a hospital bed, unable to move. I did not realize I was even there for the first three weeks. I had to endure three surgeries that totaled about twelve hours combined during my time there. And this was only the beginning of my journey. Stand behind me today and share those words of encouragement that have been a major key In helping me move on in life and keep pushing to the light at the end of the tunnel. I can only go up from here . . . I want to share a big hug with you all because you deserve it no matter who you are!

A few years ago, I kept seeing Navy SEALs in my mind during my prayer time. "Why Navy SEALs?" I wondered. As Christians, I believe we have been in training situations like Navy SEALs (but the spiritual version). So, I've been studying their training to understand the correlation. It doesn't surprise me that roughly;

Only 25% of SEAL candidates make it through Hell Week, described as the toughest training in the

US military. It involves five-and-a-half days of "cold, wet, brutally difficult operational training on fewer than four hours of sleep," the Navy says. According to the Navy, the training tests candidates' physical endurance, mental toughness, and ability to work under sleep deprivation, among other things.[1]

It's completely understandable to see how they want to "ring the bell" to signify that they are done and can't go on with the training. Please, don't ring that bell. Hang in there with everything you've got, and God will do the rest.

Former Navy SEAL Jeff Nichols suggests that one big mistake that SEAL candidates make is training to their strengths and ignoring their weaknesses.[2] Here's what the Bible says about our strengths and weaknesses and the perspective we should have:

> Even if I should choose to boast, I would not be a fool, because I would be speaking the truth. But I refrain, so no one will think more of me than is warranted by what I do or say, or because of these surpassingly great revelations. Therefore, in order to keep me from becoming conceited, I was given a thorn in my flesh, a messenger of Satan, to torment me. Three times I pleaded with the Lord to take it away from me. But he said to me, "My grace is sufficient for you, for my

power is made perfect in weakness." Therefore I will boast all the more gladly about my weaknesses, so that Christ's power may rest on me. That is why, for Christ's sake, I delight in weaknesses, in insults, in hardships, in persecutions, in difficulties. For when I am weak, then I am strong. (2 Corinthians 12:6-10).

Candidates soon learn that it is almost impossible to graduate BUD/S with a lone wolf attitude. As they endure trials together, their reliance on others is built into the training, and through support, they build confidence. The church needs to take a lesson from this and unite. We, as the church, need to lay down our agendas because only through broken hearts and complete surrender to God can we truly unite. Navy SEALs know each other so well and respect each other's unique contributions that they can maneuver as a team better than they would alone.

Also, Navy SEALs are prepared to "be in the now." They must focus! They cannot worry about yesterday or tomorrow, as it will distract their thoughts, weaken their resolve, or diminish their performance. Their team is counting on them for the successful completion of their mission. It's the same for us. Circumstances can be so overwhelming with all that's going on. Yet, the Father is asking us to have that sweet, focused communion with *Him* . . . not to look around or to the sides, but up to *Him*. As the exercises build muscles for the SEALs, our past (if we allow it) can strengthen our present situations. Even our wounds are stronger since scar tissue is tougher if, at first, sensitive.

Navy SEALs have the knowledge and specialized tools to dismantle bombs, avoid snipers and anticipate the enemy's movements. This is somewhat different from the "normal" frontline warfare in that SEALs need to be very specific with stealth and pinpoint precision. It is similar to God giving us tools (prayer, scriptures, etc.) to dismantle the bombs (trials), avoid the snipers (Satan's attacks), or anticipate the pitfalls the enemy lays for us in our own lives. There is no set formula, but His Word gives us insight into how to take one step at a time without fear of the enemy. As God is our Commander, we know His love is sufficient, and we can move forward in it!

Sometimes, I think that oppression can be so thick that it feels like we're being pushed underwater. Navy SEALs engage in strenuous underwater exercises. Phillip Francis describes the aquatic activities in his article "10 Insane Training Tests You Must Pass to Become a Navy SEAL."[3]

Every SEAL needs to know how to handle stressful situations. If they are left in rough waters, things could go wrong quick. Trainees are teamed up with another and tasked to stay underwater. Instructors will then attack them and throw them around. The instructors also mess-up their breathing equipment and they have to constantly fix that. They also can't come up for air and have to remain underwater throughout the whole exercise." In another exercise, he says, "Not drowning is pretty important for a job where 'sea' is one-third of your job description. Trainees are bound by hands and feet and thrown into a pool. They have to bob around in the water, swim certain distances, do flips underwater, and retrieve objects at the bottom of pools. They have to do all of this while completely tied up.

What's impressive is that this results in a stronger mind and body. My experience as a swimmer has taught me that any water activity increases your lung capacity. Therefore, you can stay in the water longer. You've strengthened and adapted to your surroundings.

Like Navy SEALs, the church needs to toughen up and gather strength to be an influential force in the present and the times to come. God is seeking those who're willing and courageous enough to stand for *Him*, no matter the circumstances. We can see this throughout history, but as times progressively worsen, we need to know He is in control. God will lead His army, and we can have complete trust in that! He wants soldiers willing to do the mission, despite what it may cost, even our lives if need be. Depending on where you live, this may mean different things.

American Christians have difficulty understanding what a North Korean, Chinese, or Syrian Christian endure. Their battles are severe and costly. Yet, we each have our battles; God knows where he wants us and for what length of time. He gives us the unique qualifications to fight the good fight through His grace. Will we endure the training? We need to be in the Word. We need to pray, worship, etc. And it has to be part of our daily regimen.

The Navy SEALs feel like giving in at times, but that is not an option. It's so important to be obedient, despite circumstances. There are times I don't want to pray, read the Bible, or put on worship music. However, my attitude changes and my resolve strengthens when I start any of these practices. I feel a difference. Why? I am reaching beyond my circumstances and grabbing onto God's hand. God never leaves our side. He wants us to come to Him because He's already there waiting for us. His love is that profound. He loves us enough to allow us to be broken and to use us anyway. He carries us and strengthens us through His loving grace. I keep note cards with encouraging scriptures on hand, old school cassette tapes with inspirational messages, and songs that I know will bring me back to the foot of the cross. Place these by your bed. I promise it will help you take that one step out of bed when your strength is not enough.

Another amazing thing about Navy SEALs is that they have one another's backs. We discussed community in

Chapter 2. Navy SEALs must rely on and trust each other. Their lives depend on it. Going through intense training binds them together in ways no casual activities could. They are so in sync with one another. They listen to their commander and do the next life-threatening task together. That is where we need to be as the church. As we play our parts, we must align our thoughts with our Commander, trust His judgment and strategies to overcome, and move forward, in sync, together.

We have the choice to "ring the bell" or come under the protection of our Commander, who will lift us up. The first ends our journey, while the second gives us victory and eternal hope.

> I have fought the good fight, I have finished the race, I have kept the faith. (2 Timothy 4:7 NIV)
>
> In conclusion, be strong in the Lord [be empowered through your union with Him]; draw your strength from Him [that strength which His boundless might provides]. Put on God's whole armor [the armor of a heavy-armed soldier which God supplies], that you may be able successfully to stand up against [all] the strategies and the deceits of the devil. For we are not wrestling with flesh and blood [contending only with physical opponents],

but against the despotisms, against the powers, against [the master spirits who are] the world rulers of this present darkness, against the spirit forces of wickedness in the heavenly (supernatural) sphere. Therefore put on God's complete armor, that you may be able to resist and stand your ground on the evil day [of danger], and, having done all [the crisis demands], to stand [firmly in your place]. Stand therefore [hold your ground], having tightened the belt of truth around your loins and having put on the breastplate of integrity and of moral rectitude and right standing with God, And having shod your feet in preparation [to face the enemy with the firm-footed stability, the promptness, and the readiness produced by the good news] of the Gospel of peace. Lift up over all the [covering] shield of saving faith, upon which you can quench all the flaming missiles of the wicked [one]. And take the helmet of salvation and the sword that the Spirit wields, which is the Word of God. Pray at all times (on every occasion, in every season) in the Spirit, with all [manner of] prayer and entreaty. To that end keep alert and watch with strong purpose and perseverance, interceding on behalf of all the saints (God's consecrated people). (Ephesians 6:10-18 AMPC)

Here are some of the tools we can use to fight our battles. As we just read in Ephesians 6, we are not fighting a war that is just physically circumstantial but spiritual. While praying, I had a vision of angels. They did not look like Valentine's cherubs but like soldiers with both light and rays of rainbows surrounding them. They were kneeling with their heads bowed. I asked God why I couldn't see their faces, and He replied, "That's not what you're to focus on, but your attention is to be on Me." I then observed that they held swords, but those same swords turned into Bibles. I was perplexed until God explained that the angels used God's Word for spiritual warfare. Ephesians 6:17 (NIV) states, "Take the helmet of salvation and the sword of the Spirit, which is the word of God." I never thought of it that way. When I'm in God's Word, I notice that I feel so much better equipped to move forward.

While working on my BA degree in psychology and on my master's degree, I read the writings of Freud, Jung, and many others. Truth be known, they took what the Bible states and just twisted the information. Think about Freud's thoughts on the id, ego, and superego. Thousands of years before Freud, God had already inspired writings about our flesh, soul, and spirit in His book. Having counseled hundreds of people, I can affirm that the Bible, in my humble opinion, is still the best therapeutic book that exists. God is the leading authority on the subject. And, since most of our "wars" are in our minds, what better tool to use for victory in those battles. If we are dealing with unforgiveness, God shows us how to forgive and gives us the ability to do it.

Are you struggling with rejection? Jesus knew the ultimate rejection on the cross. Even the night before His crucifixion, He found His friends sleeping when they should have been awake and praying with and for Him. Also, God instructs us extensively on the topic of fear. The phrase "fear not" appears over eighty times in the Bible. So, if we want to win the battle before us, we have to get proficient at using the "Sword of the Spirit." Read the Bible. If you can, participate in a Bible study.

Worship is another wonderful tool! Through counseling survivors of Satanic ritual abuse, I learned that the enemy hates worship. Worshiping God opposes everything Satan stands for. In fact, in Matthew 4:10 (NIV), when the devil is trying to tempt Jesus in the desert, Jesus says to him, "Away from me, Satan! For it is written: 'Worship the Lord your God, and serve him only.'" Yeah, that didn't sit well with our enemy.

When we worship God, it opens the doors to an even more intimate fellowship with Him. Look at this verse by itself and the hope we have in Him. There is every reason to worship Him, knowing He cares so intimately for us. "LORD, you are my God; I will exalt you and praise your name, for in perfect faithfulness you have done wonderful things, things planned long ago." (Isaiah 25:1 NIV).

In John 10:10 (NIV), we read that "the thief comes only to steal and kill and destroy," but Jesus states, "I have come that they may have life, and have it to the full." Now read this: "Sing to God, sing in praise of His name, extol Him who rides on the clouds; rejoice before Him—His name is the Lord. A Father to the fatherless, a defender of widows, is God in his holy dwelling" (Psalm 68:4-5 NIV).

Why wouldn't we want to worship God who loves us so dearly? And in that time of worship, we are also fighting the enemy. David knew the power of worship very well. We know David as the kid who fought against Goliath and, as an adult, committed adultery with Bathsheba. He even had her husband murdered. David was not perfect and knew his strength only came from God. When many wanted to attack him, he turned to God as his defender. When he was extremely depressed, David turned to God to be his healer and redeemer. When he was weak and sinned, he asked forgiveness and accepted the consequences. Whatever battle he faced, he knew God would be the one to help give him victory over it. We see this throughout the Psalms.

In 2 Chronicles, we read that Jehoshaphat worshiped God and fought a war that seemed impossible. Jehoshaphat was a righteous man before God. Long story short, the Moabites, Ammonites, and some of the Meunites wanted to attack his army. Not just one group but three groups were rallying against him! I can see why he wanted to call on the Lord. This was God's response:

Then the Spirit of the Lord came on Jahaziel son of Zechariah, the son of Benaiah, the son of Jeiel, the son of Mattaniah, a Levite and descendant of Asaph, as he stood in the assembly. He said: "Listen, King Jehoshaphat and all who live in Judah and Jerusalem! This is what the LORD says to you: 'Do not be afraid or discouraged because of this vast army. For the battle is not yours, but God's. Tomorrow march down against them. They will be climbing up by the Pass of Ziz, and you will find them at the end of the gorge in the Desert of Jeruel. You will not have to fight this battle. Take up your positions; stand firm and see the deliverance the LORD will give you, Judah and Jerusalem. Do not be afraid; do not be discouraged. Go out to face them tomorrow, and the LORD will be with you.' Jehoshaphat bowed down with his face to the ground, and all the people of Judah and Jerusalem fell down in worship before the LORD. Then some Levites from the Kohathites and Korahites stood up and praised the LORD, the God of Israel, with a very loud voice. Early in the morning they left for the Desert of Tekoa. As they set out, Jehoshaphat stood and said, "Listen to me, Judah and people of Jerusalem! Have faith in the LORD your God and you will be upheld; have faith in his prophets and you will be successful." After consulting the people, Jehoshaphat appointed men to sing to the LORD and to praise him for the splendor of his holiness as they went out at the head of the army, saying: "Give thanks to the LORD, for his love endures forever." (2 Chronicles 20:14-21 NIV)

So instead of a physical battle that seemed impossible, God had them worship, and they were victorious! That is the same God that is our God! He will give us victory! Let us worship God.

Another powerful tool we need to use in battle is prayer. Admittedly, I love to pray. I love to pray using scripture since it is God's own promises to us. Prayer interrupts Satan's plans. I recall working with an inmate who left the occult. He told me the occult hated when Christians prayed. They could tell that people were praying during their horrific ceremonies because they would literally see angels. Yeah, this is deep and powerful. Why do I believe what he said? Because I counseled others who were not diagnosed as delusional, didn't know each other, and didn't use hallucinogenic drugs but shared similar experiences. I could have chalked it up to coincidence. But seeing their body language, I could tell they truly believed what they were sharing with me. It makes perfect sense since even Jesus prayed frequently. Therefore, we need to pray!

To understand our next weapon of warfare, we must first read this story.

Then one of the crowd answered and said, "Teacher, I brought You my son, who has a mute spirit. And wherever it seizes him, it throws him down; he foams at the mouth, gnashes his teeth, and becomes rigid. So I spoke to Your disciples, that they should cast it out, but they could not." He answered him and said, "O faithless generation, how long shall I be with you? How long shall I bear with you? Bring him to Me." Then they brought him to Him. And when he saw Him, immediately the spirit convulsed him, and he fell on the ground and wallowed, foaming at the mouth. So He asked his father, "How long has this been happening to him?" And he said, "From childhood. And often he has thrown him both into the fire and into the water to destroy him. But if You can do anything, have compassion on us and help us." Jesus said to him, "If you can believe, all things *are* possible to him who believes." Immediately the father of the child cried out and said with tears, "Lord, I believe; help my unbelief!" When Jesus saw that the people came running together, He rebuked the unclean spirit, saying to it, "Deaf and dumb spirit, I command you, come out of him and enter him no more!" Then *the spirit* cried out, convulsed him greatly, and came out of him. And he became as one dead, so that many said, "He is dead." But

Jesus took him by the hand and lifted him up, and he arose. And when He had come into the house, His disciples asked Him privately, "Why could we not cast it out?" So He said to them, "This kind can come out by nothing but prayer and fasting." (Mark 9:17-29 NKJV)

The keyword from that story is "*fasting.*" "Fasting, according to the Bible, means to voluntarily reduce or eliminate your intake of food for a specific time and purpose."[4] When you give up eating, don't put on a sad face like the hypocrites."[4] It is referring to Matthew 6:16. Fasting was used in battle several times throughout the Bible. Daniel engaged in fasting, and after twenty-one days, the archangel Michael appeared. It is important to note that Daniel lived in the highly complex time of Nebuchadnezzar. I won't go into the whole story, but if you're not familiar with it, I encourage you to read the book of Daniel. Nebuchadnezzar was the Hitler of the Bible. He was horrific.

Another story is from the book of Esther. Our unlikely heroine is an orphaned girl who was kidnapped by the king's soldiers to be presented with many other women to be a potential bride. It doesn't sound like much fun, right? I'm sure she felt loneliness, fear, and maybe even righteous anger. Yet, God had huge plans for her. An evil man named Haman wanted to commit genocide on the Jews. Esther, herself, was Jewish. Long story short, she fasted for three days and asked for a meal with the king, which was granted. At that meal, she exposed Haman, won favor with the king, and the Jews were saved. Prayer and fasting opened unique doors that changed history. It still can and does. Fasting can be done just by you, or it can be corporately as a whole church. An entire country can be called to fast, as when Abraham Lincoln proclaimed March 30, 1863 a national day of prayer and fasting. Here is a portion of the Proclamation.

By the President of the United States of America. A Proclamation.

Whereas, the Senate of the United States, devoutly recognizing the Supreme Authority and just Government of Almighty God, in all the affairs of men and of nations, has, by a resolution, requested the President to designate and set apart a day for National prayer and humiliation.

And whereas it is the duty of nations as well as of men, to own their dependence upon the overruling power of God, to confess their sins and transgressions, in humble sorrow, yet with assured hope that genuine repentance will lead to mercy and pardon; and to recognize the sublime truth, announced in the Holy

Scriptures and proven by all history, that those nations only are blessed whose God is the Lord."[5]

This very act of fasting would also forever change the Civil War and history. It would be a war that would end slavery.

In Esther, it is written, "Who knows but that you have come to your royal position for such a time as this?" (Esther 4:14 NIV). God knows the tools He's given you, so believe in His power to see victories and triumphs happen! He chose us to fight this battle, and all we need to do is ask which direction to go. Harriet Tubman, who helped save many enslaved people and had been enslaved herself, asked God which way to go when she was helping people escape the horrors of slavery. He told her left, right, through the river, or other directions. Not one enslaved person perished, and that war was won.

And sometimes, we just need to rest and "be still" and remember that God fights our battles. "He makes wars cease to the ends of the earth. He breaks the bow and shatters the spear; he burns the shields with fire. He says, 'Be still, and know that I am God; I will be exalted among the nations, I will be exalted in the earth'" (Psalm 46:9-10 NIV).

Ultimately, God wins! The victory is His! Therefore, no matter how hard things may become, keep in mind that if we are with Him, we will see victory too. Revelation 11:15 (ESV) says: "Then the seventh angel then blew his trumpet, and there were loud voices in heaven, saying, 'The kingdom of the world has become the kingdom of our Lord and of His Christ, and He shall reign forever and ever.'"

Amen!

Endnotes

1   Alia Shoaib, "A Navy SEAL candidate died and another was hospitalized after grueling 'Hell Week' training," February 6, 2022, https://www.businessinsider. com/navy-seal-candidate-dies-another-hospitalized-after-hell-week-2022-2.

2   Tim Kirkpatrick, "9 of the biggest mistakes sailors make while at BUD/S," May 14, 2018, https://www.wearethemighty.com/popular/most-common-buds-mistakes/.

3   "10 Insane Training Tests You Must Pass to Become a Navy Seal," June 8, 2018, https://allmymedicine.com/Fitness/10-Insane-Training-Tests-You-Must-Pass-to-Become-a-Navy-Seal/.

4   "Fasting and Prayer," https://harmonyfellowshipny.com/fasting-and-prayer/.

5   "Proclamation Appointing a National Fast Day," http://www.abrahamlincolnonline. org/lincoln/speeches/fast.htm.

CHAPTER 6

SPIRITUAL DEPRESSION, JOY, & HOPE

There is so much fear, confusion, and exhaustion everywhere. News is presented as "Breaking News" even if it's not; the red banner on the screen forces our minds into emergency mode: fight or flight. National and international crises added to our distress can drive us to the verge of paralyzing overload. Broken relationships or struggling ones with overwhelming circumstances that seem to have no solution, loneliness, etc. I could go on and on, but there's a great deal to process. If you're not dealing with trials, you undoubtedly know loved ones who are. So many are "doing their best" but feel like they're hitting a wall, and prayers sometimes go unanswered. With all my heart, I do believe there is *hope*! I've studied history for years now and wondered how people survived difficult times. Even now, in observing survivors around the world, I found something amazing. I see this as a common thread among many—an eternal belief that rises above circumstances and lifts you higher.

We've all experienced times during which we wanted the world to swallow us up or

better yet, to be beamed up to heaven. Jesus experienced it in the most profound ways. He understands the sufferings of every one of us. Jesus was beaten until His flesh fell off. A crown of thorns was jammed onto His head. Nails were pounded through His wrists and feet. Lastly, as He hung on a cross, He slowly suffocated. It's unfathomable. Yet, I believe His emotional pain even surpassed His physical pain.

A week before, Jesus had ridden through a cheering crowd, knowing that those same people would turn on Him. He endured Gethsemane alone, crying and sweating blood, which meant that the stress on Him was unimaginable. Then, as He was dying, Jesus was taunted and ridiculed mercilessly. Why would He endure that for you, for me? He could have stopped it at any time, but His purpose was to defeat Death for our sake. His love for us is immeasurable. He suffered for us all. I sometimes want to rush through Holy Week to get to Easter because I hate thinking about how Jesus suffered. However, during that week, I'm reminded that He laid His life down for you, me, and us all. Sometimes, I feel unworthy to come before Him, but He says to us all, "come to me just as you are." His love is authentic. His grace and mercy are more than sufficient. I pray that you feel His love and acceptance when you've been rejected by people. I pray that you know He's always with you when you feel lonely. You are so loved!

We understand that Jesus endured physical and mental torment far more so than we ever will. He also had a more complete spiritual understanding than we ever will. Our experiences, then, can lead us into something called spiritual depression. Spiritual depression feels a lot like chemical depression, and in some ways, it is. It can coincide and be exacerbated by chemical depression but not always. And before I go any further, please seek immediate help if the depth of your depression has reached a level of considering suicide. Depression of a spiritual nature may make you want to be beamed up to heaven, to want to go to our eternal home, however, it won't make you think of ways to act out suicidal thoughts or want to end your life.

Even when people follow God, they experience some level of spiritual depression at one time or another. It feels as if you're drifting away from the faith, when, in reality, you're learning how to draw nearer to God. It's a time of questioning whether He exists or not because the pain is so deep. Trials can accompany it but not always. You feel like you are in the deepest pit and are unsure how to get out of it.

You are not alone if you have experienced or are experiencing depression such as this. People of great faith have dealt with it. By reading the Psalms, we know David wrote about his pain, confusion, frustration, and loneliness. Jonah ran away from his calling, and Elijah hid in a cave. The books of Jeremiah and Job are all about spiritual agony.

Then there are people like Mother Teresa who wrote letters about how she felt God had abandoned her. Corrie ten Boom, who helped save many Jews during the Holocaust, wrote about questioning God when she was in the concentration camp. Nick Vujicic, born without limbs, talks about how he struggled with hopelessness, but God has used him to encourage thousands worldwide.

If you talk with any spiritual leaders, they will tell you it can be a very lonely walk. Here's the deal, faith cannot become real until we own it. What does that mean? If everything goes well and easily in our lives, we are not challenged. An easy faith tends to be a weak faith that is based on circumstances rather than tried and true, tested in fire, faith—having built trust in a God who loves us so much that He sent His son to die on our behalf. He wants us to know His intimate and redemptive love above all else.

He gives us gifts and blessings daily to demonstrate that love to us. Each breath we take is a gift from God. But it's not because of those things that we should love Him back. He deserves our love because He does, not because of what He does. Also, we can't just believe in God because someone told us it's the right thing to do or follow the crowd. Our faith is an intimate dance with Him; a personal relationship with Him.

I love the Song of Solomon (a book in the Bible) because God shows us His love for the church through two lovers.

Granted, I am glad my husband has not complimented me, "Your hair is like a flock of goats descending from the hills of Gilead" (Song of Solomon 4:1 NIV) as did Solomon to his lover. I am sure it was very appropriate for the time, but a "flock of goats" doesn't stir up a vision of beautiful hair. Yet, when you understand the intimate love language between these two people and realize that God's love for us is so profound, you understand why He is a jealous God. He wants our full attention. And sometimes, that means us being at the very end of ourselves. No flesh can get in the way because we are exhausted, and all we can do sometimes is to lie prostrate or even curled up before Him. Tears may flow, or we may pound fists into a pillow. Our prayers may sound more like moans and heartfelt cries. It may even feel like God has departed from us and left us there alone.

The truth is that God has not abandoned us. He wants us to know the depth of His comfort and care, joy, and love. First, read Psalm 42 NIV.

As the deer pants for streams of water, so my soul pants for you, my God. My soul thirsts for God, for the living God. When can I go and meet with God? My tears have been my food day and night, while people say to me all day long, "Where is your God?" These things I remember as I pour out my soul: how I used to go to the house of God under the protection of the Mighty One with shouts of joy and praise among the festive throng.

Why, my soul, are you downcast? Why so disturbed within me? Put your hope in God, for I will yet praise him, my Savior and my God.

My soul is downcast within me; therefore I will remember you from the land of the Jordan, the heights of Hermon—from Mount Mizar. Deep calls to deep in the roar of your waterfalls; all your waves and breakers have swept over me.

By day the LORD directs his love, at night his song is with me— a prayer to the God of my life.

I say to God my Rock, "Why have you forgotten me? Why must I go about mourning, oppressed by the enemy?" My bones suffer mortal agony as my foes taunt me, saying to me all day long, "Where is your God?"

Why, my soul, are you downcast? Why so disturbed within me? Put your hope in God, for I will yet praise him, my Savior and my God.

Now read this single but powerful verse:

"Cast your burden on the LORD, and he will sustain you; he will never permit the righteous to be moved." (Psalm 55:22 ESV)

And now this:

"Because he holds fast to me in love, I will deliver him; I will protect him, because he knows my name. When he calls to me, I will answer him; I will be with him in trouble; I will rescue him and honor him." (Psalm 91:14-15 ESV)

The previous list of scriptures describes how He will not leave you but will sustain you. In addition, you will overcome with God's grace. "How?" you ask. Be honest with God. He knows you. "You know when I sit down or stand up. You know my thoughts even when I'm far away" (Psalm 139:2 NLT). And here is something I've been studying more, "Humble yourselves before the Lord, and He will lift you up" (James 4:10 NIV). When we rest in Him and surrender, He can lift us to another level of spirituality, which means understanding more of His love and will.

To escape the depths of darkness, we need to recognize that worry and fear usually hold us back. Worry and fear steal our present and future joy and do nothing constructively to make life good. With all that's happened in yours and my lifetime, it's easy to worry about or fear the future. Yet, I know that I get filled up when I pray, worship, and am in the Word. My perspective changes and hope returns. In our weakness, God is strong! Look what He's carried you and I through already. He won't stop now. Here are some scriptures to meditate on:

My flesh and heart may fail, but God is the strength of my heart, and my portion forever. (Psalm 73:26 NIV)

Don't be afraid, for I am with you. Don't be discouraged, for I am your God. I will strengthen you and help you. I will hold you up with my victorious right hand. (Isaiah 41:10 NLT)

Think of that image! We may envision all the burdens on our shoulders, but God can hold us and all burdens in His loving hand. He won't let us go, and He will carry us until we're home with Him.

I love this quote by Marjorie Pay Hinckley: "The trick is to enjoy life. Don't wish away your days, waiting for better ones ahead. No matter how tough the day is, there is always something good about it."[1] It's so easy to think, "Life will be great when . . ." It is more of a fight to live in the now because life isn't fair in many ways, and that will not change. Unfairness and trials will always exist. I'm the first to admit I would love a life with no trials, but I understand and still strive to strive for this: "I have fought the good fight, I have finished the race, I have kept the faith" (2 Timothy 4:7 NIV). A race is won with endurance and perseverance.

The obstacle before you may look insanely challenging, but I believe that's where God gives us the strength and not a moment ahead or later. He gives us exactly what we need to fight the good fight. We want to jump over it to the future, but we would miss the strength, patience, and joy we can get through the obstacle. I understand growing weary; there are times in the past as recent as yesterday when I wanted to stop because I'm tired. Giving up would have meant missing out on so many amazing things in life. All we're responsible for is taking one more step, enjoying the ability to be moving forward, and knowing there will be good things ahead, despite the trials.

You may have already survived spiritual depression, or you may be going through it now. And you may experience it multiple times. Truth be known, "this too shall pass," and you will experience deeper joy and victory in God when this season of your life ends if you persevere. After the "dark night of the soul," you will clearly see the love He has for you. God doesn't punish us but disciples us because He is a loving Father. Hebrews 12:11 (AMP) explains this process and outcome well:

> For the time being no discipline brings joy, but seems sad and painful; yet to those who have been trained by it, afterwards it yields the peaceful fruit of righteousness [right standing with God and a lifestyle and attitude that seeks conformity to God's will and purpose].

Here are some other scriptures to consider:

Then Job answered the LORD and said: "I know that you can do all things, and that no purpose of yours can be restrained." (Job 42:1-2 AMP)

For I consider that the sufferings of this present time are not worth comparing with the glory that is to be revealed to us . . . And we know that for those who love God all things work together for good, for those who are called according to his purpose. (Romans 8:18, 28 ESV)

Jesus looked at them and said, "With man it is impossible, but not with God; all things are possible with God." (Mark 10:27 NIV)

Pay attention to one of the most powerful and encouraging scripture passages.

We are afflicted in every way, but not crushed; perplexed, but not driven to despair; persecuted, but not forsaken; struck down, but not destroyed; always carrying in the body the death of Jesus, so that the life of Jesus may also be manifested in our bodies. For we who live are always being given over to death for Jesus' sake, so that the life of Jesus also may be manifested in our mortal flesh. So death is at work in us, but life in you.

Since we have the same spirit of faith according to what has been written, "I believed, and so I spoke," we also believe, and so we also speak, knowing that he who raised the Lord Jesus will raise us also with Jesus and bring us with you into his presence. For it is all for your sake, so that as grace extends to more and more people it may increase thanksgiving, to the glory of God.

So we do not lose heart. Though our outer self is wasting away, our inner self is being renewed day by day. For this light momentary affliction is preparing for us an eternal weight of glory beyond all comparison, as we look not to the things that are seen but to the things that are unseen. For the things that are seen are transient, but the things that are unseen are eternal. (2 Corinthians 4:8-18 ESV)

Endnotes

1 https://www.goodreads.com/quotes/159315-the-trick-is-to-enjoy-life-don-t-wish-away-your.

CHAPTER 7

REST, RESTORATION, & REDEMPTION

Like many of you, I am no stranger to loss, having become well acquainted through experiences in my life. I've experienced pain I would have rather avoided, but it's real, and it's the life God has given me. That's why I'm sure He must never tire of hearing prayers for the three R's: rest, restoration, and redemption. I've been confused and even downhearted when these prayers didn't get answered. How can God not want this for His children?

I have expectations of Him and how my life should have looked. Some of my life looks like I thought it would, but more of it bears no resemblance whatsoever. Expectations, specifically unfulfilled expectations, can shake our faith. They are, however, an unstable foundation on which to rest our faith. God is ever-present, unshakable, and in control.

REST

"Rest is not idleness, and to lie sometimes on the grass on a summer day listening to the murmur of water, or watching the clouds float across the sky, is hardly a waste of time," said John Lubbock.[1]

Our bodies require rest for homeostasis. We know we can't function well without restorative sleep. We sometimes feel guilty about "chilling out," but it's necessary, and not just physically. We need to rest mentally as well. I won't go into all the ways to do it, but one beneficial way is to pray. I recall being instructed by the doctors not to pray while I was having a procedure to scan my brain. The neurologist explained it would alter the readings because of the increased positive hormonal changes prayer causes in the brain.

There is scientific evidence that prayer does increase the levels of neuropeptides our brain produces. Dr. Andrew Newberg says, "We see not only changes in the activity levels, but in different neurotransmitters, the chemicals in our brain."[2] And if we understand prayer being communication with our loving Father, it's not hard to imagine that He designed it like that on purpose. He made it good for us to pray in more ways than one. In the process of aligning ourselves with His will spiritually through prayer, we are being physically and mentally reinvigorated as well. We should always trust Him to have His best interest for us. Isaiah 40:28-31 (NIV) is a beautiful example of this.

> Do you not know? Have you not heard? The LORD is the everlasting God, the Creator of the ends of the earth. He will not grow tired or weary, and his understanding no one can fathom. He gives strength to the weary and increases the power of the weak. Even youths grow tired and weary, and young men stumble and fall; but those who hope in the LORD will renew their strength. They will soar on wings like eagles; they will run and not grow weary, they will walk and not faint.

I've read how eagles will fly into strong winds to find the lift they need to soar effortlessly. And with their eyesight, the view from up there must be incredible, right? So, rest in the arms of our loving Father and hope in Him so He can renew your strength.

RESTORATION

I always thought "restoration" returns things to their original state, but it's different. In the book of Joel, I love how God replaces the crops locusts eat. In the book of Ruth, Naomi lost her husband and both of her sons. No one could replace those losses. Yet, due to Ruth's obedience to God in following her mother-in-law Naomi, she bore a baby (Obed) with her new husband. This child was a direct lineage to Jesus (Obed to Jesse to David to Jesus). The book of Job describes Job's many devastating losses. Despite his circumstances, he remained faithful to God and was doubly blessed (Job 42:10-17). All three—Naomi, Ruth, and Job—grieved their losses deeply. Restoration requires and follows loss, which can take on many forms: death, divorce, friendship, health, finances, dreams, etc.

Yesterday was Nikki's birthday. Twenty-five years ago, she was the baby we were in the process of adopting. She was part of our family for fifteen months until her birth mom decided she wanted her back. Thankfully, we were allowed to see her occasionally as she grew up. However, thirteen years ago, fearing her daughter would find out that she had put her up for adoption, Nikki's mother ended our visitations. When she was twelve years old, we met for the last time as she was wheeled out of another one of her open-heart surgeries. Instinctively, she placed her hand on my cheek as I bent over her bed. It was a habit she had started the day we met her when she was three weeks old. My heart broke.

Nikki had been grafted into our hearts from the first moments we saw her and is as dear to us as our birth children. We went through five open-heart surgeries with her. We saw her take her first steps, held her as she teethed, loved her laughter, cuddled her through difficult medical complications, etc. It was a very deep loss. Part of our heart is still missing. Yet, I recently found out she loves rainbows and feels "someone's watching over her." Jim and I have never stopped praying for her. Is this all coincidental? Absolutely not. It's beauty for ashes (Isaiah 61:3) because despite her going back to her birth mom, we see that we made an impact when we raised her for part of her life.

Another restoration story happened when our daughter-in-law, Dorothea, read a story in my first book about our first daughter who passed away at four and a half months old. Dorothea realized that their birthdays were only two months apart and that they would have been the same age. She told me that now I would know what it's like to have a daughter that age. Again, one person cannot replace the loss of another, but there can be sweet healing. Talk about a kind of Ruth/Naomi situation.

One other amazing story of restoration was a miracle I saw in Poland. I stood there looking at my audience, and I could feel my heart racing. Who was I to talk at a church in Poland, whose people have a history of enduring Communism and Nazism? I took a deep breath and looked at the woman appointed to be my Polish translator. She nodded, and I began to say what God had laid on my heart.

You see, our trip to Poznan, Poland, had been delayed three years by then. We had been so excited about going there after building an incredible connection with the church's pastor, and then boom, our plans crashed abruptly. We didn't have the opportunity to address that church for another three years, as the pastor had wanted initially.

It's a wonderful church because they serve Jewish survivors of the Holocaust as well as their children and grandchildren. On their altar, is a menorah—a six-branched candelabra symbolic for Jews. They are located off the street, camouflaged by the buildings in front and to the sides. The contrast of gray Communist-built buildings and the new architecture with many colors was a reminder of the history and perseverance of the Polish people.

The pastor explained how communists took over his childhood home for their headquarters. One of his toys, he remembered, was a grenade they had left behind. He and his cousin uncovered human bones buried in their backyard as they dug a garden. He took us to a military cemetery where we saw the graves of American soldiers and all those who allied with Poland. This trip included visits to Auschwitz, Anne Frank's home, Corrie ten Boom's hiding place, and Checkpoint Charlie. We were also able to visit my great-grandma Kalas's apartment that barely survived the horrors of the war and the church in which she played the organ until she left just before World War II started in earnest. She used to tell us of the impact Hitler's speeches had on her and everyone else at the time.

Thoughts ran through my head of the picture my family keeps of my great-grandpa kneeling for prayer and communion with other soldiers in the rubble of an English church that had been bombed in World War I. He returned to the states and became a pastor. With my other great-grandma Pickering (her maiden name was Schwartz), he started the first all-Jewish Boy Scout troop in Chicago, Illinois, during World War II, while the enemies across the sea were trying to eradicate the Jews. I felt the burden of carrying on the generational calling to bring the love of God to others. And now, here I was in a foreign country, asked to share a message of hope. I didn't feel worthy, but I knew that whatever I shared would have to be from God.

God impressed on my heart that I was supposed to speak about the loss of our daughter. Until then, this was the most challenging trial I had ever endured, making it seem different to discuss our loss in a country where they had lost friends, whole families, and even neighborhoods. They couldn't hold their children while they died like I was able to do. In addition, they had seen many people tortured. I never felt more inadequate, but, you see, God knew I was to be there for such a time. His love is in the details.

A little boy had been born the year we were initially supposed to go to Poland. He was three years old at the time. We did make it to Europe but we never had the pleasure of meeting this sweet child on earth as he died unexpectedly a few days before we arrived. The surreal thing is that I had been scheduled to speak there the weekend before, but the church had other visitors. Our plans were flexible, so we postponed our visit by one week. Waiting one more week to speak there was part of God's plan, and we didn't even realize that until it all happened. The little boy's parents were not present that week before when their son was still alive. But, following his death, the parents and older son attended the service at which I was speaking.

I walked up to the altar of the church. My heart was beating so fast and I muttered prayers under my breath. The pastor had asked me to give a spontaneous message to the church's children about the loss of their little friend. Standing there, feeling entirely incompetent, I looking into all of those sad eyes set in such innocent faces. "Heaven is like the best park you've ever been to and even better than that! Jesus is there holding your brother and friend close to His heart.", I began. A few minutes later the whole congregation was crying, and I lost my first translator to her tears and inability to continue. Only by God's grace was I able to maintain my composure. Another church member came up to translate for me. When I started to speak about our experience with our daughter, she gave way to her tears as well and had to discontinue. So, our friend, the pastor, had to translate himself. His shaky hand grasped the microphone and he looked at me, with tears in his eyes, awaiting what I was going to say next. It was apparent how real and raw this was for all those involved. My heart ached for them, and I longed to bring them a glimmer of hope. I wanted them to feel the same hope I had experienced that kept me living after my daughter went to her eternal home.

I said, "It's not about how hard you pray that keeps someone alive or motivates God to answer. God gives and takes away, and we don't always understand, but He sees the bigger picture and has a more comprehensive plan than we can know." The pastors' shoulders dropped as if a huge burden had been lifted off. This was an important message I needed to share because Jim and I had been told by people that we didn't pray hard enough, and that's why Elizabeth died. I wrote this in my first book, *The Raindrops on the Windshield Sound Like Popcorn*:

"I was still holding guilt in my heart for Elizabeth's condition. People had told me that maybe I hadn't prayed hard enough or said the right words or had enough faith, or that maybe she had been punished for my own sin. Even though I knew these things were untrue, I questioned it as a mother . . . in my heart."

Jim and I had studied theology on this topic and knew it in our minds, but I needed to hold that confirmation continually in my heart. When our daughter, Jessica, was born, she coded. She was immediately transferred to PICU where the heart tests began.

We were reliving what we had gone through with Elizabeth. However, this story in our lives would have a different outcome. Jessica's heart is healthy! Jessica was with us on that trip to Poland and is an adult now. Elizabeth received the ultimate healing, but Jessica received a miracle here on earth. When I shared this, the pastor broke down and cried as well. I understood why. This church prayed with everything in them for this little boy to live. God loves our children more than we do, which seems unfathomable, but it's true. So here I was, a woman from the United States, bringing a message of love from God in His timing.

At first, I didn't understand why we had to wait to go to Poland, but then it all came together. It was especially meaningful when I went to hug a stranger with whom I shared the pain no mother should have to experience. We hugged tightly and wept. I could feel her pain and it hit my heart. We understood each other. I wanted to confirm her belief that God loves us even when circumstances are at their worst. Waleria, the boy's mom, and I connected immediately, as do most parents who have lost a child. God cared not only for that church but also for each individual. His love is so deep and amazing. His timing is perfectly ordained.

Restoration is so much more than returning things to their previous state. I think it's so much sweeter because it gives you a different perspective. As I write this, the world is experiencing the aforementioned pandemic. I am a hugger, and I miss hugging people like crazy. When this is all over, anyone near me may have to peel me off them (sorry for the image to any non-hugger readers getting the heebie-jeebies right now). So, when I opened our front door and was surprised by our son, Josh, whom we hadn't seen for a while due to travel restrictions and canceled trips, I lost it. I mean, I seriously let out a loud cry of deep joy. I didn't even realize to what extent I was holding it all in. I knew I missed him but wow! This was a glimpse of what was to come. It was hope. It reminded me of what we have to look forward to in heaven—our ultimate homecoming.

I don't think complete restoration always happens here on earth either. If things were perfect, we wouldn't long for a new heaven and a new earth, as the Bible describes. Yet, when we rest in Him and allow God to hold us (Isaiah 41:10), He will bring deep joy and peace that surpasses circumstances. I also believe that the kind of restoration He brings is for a bigger picture—one we may not understand until we see Him face to face. Our pain is never wasted. Even Naomi and Job were in positions where he "cursed the day of his birth" (Job 3:1 AMP), or she felt that God caused her bitterness as we can see in (Ruth 1:20 NIV). I know I've "fought" with God about why He didn't answer my prayers at times the way I hoped. Yet, I can share story after story about how Romans 8:28 (NIV) is true: "And we know that in all things God works for the good of those who love him, who have been called according to his purpose." Powerful! Not my will, but His will be done.

And after you have suffered a little while, the God of all grace, who has called you to his eternal glory in Christ, will himself restore, confirm, strengthen, and establish you. (1 Peter 5:10 ESV)

REDEMPTION

If you look back at your life and see how God carried you through and provided miracles, you will gain strength and hope to endure any present trials. I read once that you're either at a point when you're at the end of a trial, in the middle, or at the beginning. At our present time, there is so much adversity. In the midst of it all, God is faithful. Yet, when you've lost something, what's most important is a renewed hope and strength.

We don't put on sackcloth or throw ashes on ourselves like they did in ancient times, but we experience deep mourning over loved ones, lost relationships, loss of health or jobs or dreams just the same. Job walked in obedience stating that "God's plans will not be thwarted." Obedience (waiting on God and trusting Him) brings redemption. Job did get double blessings, but I'm sure he still grieved the loss of loved ones. He knew if he trusted God, he would get even closer to Him. Job didn't even know why he was going through his trials. It's wild to think that Job didn't have the advantage of knowing that God came in the flesh to demonstrate His love for us since Jesus wouldn't be born for several hundred more years.

Unlike Job, we have a New Testament promising us 1) eternal life through Jesus since our sins are washed away (ultimate redemption there) and 2) that nothing will separate us from the love of Christ. I'm not going to pretend I understand why specific trials occur or even suffering happens at times, but I do know God is our Redeemer. Even so, Job exclaimed, "For I know that my Redeemer lives." (Job 19:25 ESV)

Here is another promise: "For I consider that the sufferings of this present time are not worth comparing with the glory that is to be revealed to us" (Romans 8:18 ESV).

I don't believe in karma. The following statement would cause it to kick my behind if I did. Bad things happen to good people, and good things happen to bad people. Yes, there are consequences for our actions, but some "get away with murder" while others are genuinely kind and still deal with tough trials. I do think obedience, despite circumstances, makes a huge difference in character. I love these verses: ". . . but we rejoice in our sufferings, knowing that suffering produces endurance, and endurance produces character, and character produces hope" (Romans 5:3-4 ESV).

I will be honest and say I don't always rejoice when suffering. Well, not right away. However, if I look back, I see I've allowed trials to build character rather than grow bitter. I realize I've gotten stronger and still have hope, despite the circumstances. It doesn't mean my obedience caused the trials to go the way I wanted them to go. However, they did produce positive results.

Here is another beloved verse: "But the fruit of the Spirit [the result of His presence within us] is love [unselfish concern for others], joy, [inner] peace, patience [not the ability to wait, but how we act while waiting], kindness, goodness, faithfulness, gentleness, self-control. Against such things there is *no law*" (Galatians 5:22-23 AMP, emphasis added). So, consider karma. Just in case you were waiting for karma to get back at an enemy, here's an answer for that: "Never take your own revenge, beloved, but leave room for the wrath of God, for it is written, '*vengeance is mine, I will repay,*' says the Lord" (Romans 12:19 NASB, emphasis added). God's wrath versus karma? No competition there.

God is a God of rest, restoration, and redemption. His promises are throughout His Word. Be encouraged that He has the best in His plans for you.

Endnotes
1 https://www.brainyquote.com/quotes/john_lubbock_107976.
2 "Power of Prayer: What Happens to Your Brain When You Pray?" December 23, 2014, https://www.nbcnews.com/news/religion/power-prayer-what-happens-your-brain-when-you-pray-n273956.

CHAPTER 8

GOD'S LOVE

Many of us understand the love of God, having been taught verses like John 3:16 or having learned songs with lyrics like, "Oh, how I love Jesus . . . because He first loved me." As I mentioned previously, there was a pivotal moment in my life when the love of our Father became very personal for me. In my first book, *The Raindrops on the Windshield Sound Like Popcorn,* I wrote about that time:

A few weeks after Elizabeth died, I went to the gravesite and just broke down. The pain was so intense, like none I had felt before. I asked God if He understood how I felt. Did He know how bad my arms ached to hold her? In the gentlest way, I felt Him say, "Yes, I watched my Son die." I understood Easter before Elizabeth died, but I gained a deeper understanding of it after she died. Death is inevitable. So is eternity. It just comes down to where we are going to spend it. Everything I have learned and experienced points to a Savior, a God who loves us fully and unconditionally.

God takes us by the hand (or carries us, like in the poem "Footprints in the Sand") as we face considerable and sometimes devastating challenges. God's love for us is absolute and never changes. It is a universal truth. People and circumstances may confuse our understanding of God's love. These are not always good gauges of His love for us, but sometimes, people tend to look to them for validation. I've done it myself. People will let us down, circumstances will turn ugly, and we may not feel God's love for us. The keyword in that sentence is "feel." God's love is not based on His mood or our performance; it's true all the time and regardless of our circumstances. Here's the deal: no one is perfect, except God. We cannot expect anyone or anything to fill us the way He does or as completely as only He can.

We see God's love in the big events of life, but His expression of love is even in the little details as well. My friend Debra made me a beautiful quilt a few years ago, which reminded me that the God of the universe is interested in our details and cares to reveal Himself in uniquely meaningful ways. Here's her story.

I wanted to give you a meaningful gift for the end of the year because I had been your Secret Pal. I knew you loved rainbows, and I knew of your great physical challenges. I can't remember if I knew you liked butterflies or not. Anyway, I could clearly see in my mind a quilted butterfly made of rainbow colors. Then God gave me this scripture to sew onto the quilt, Job 19:25-27 (NIV): "I know that my Redeemer lives, and that in the end he will stand on the earth. And after my skin has been destroyed, yet in my flesh I will see God. I myself will see him with my own eyes—I, and not another. How my heart yearns within me!" It seemed to fit perfectly as the reality of all the symbolism of the butterfly and the rainbow (and more) will be fulfilled in the end.

Debra didn't know that the verse was the very scripture I had chosen to meditate on throughout that year. Also, she had never seen my artwork, which was done in rainbow watercolors outlined with a black Sharpie. Not even knowing that latter part, she felt she needed to add black piping around the butterfly (which clinched things for me). To me, butterflies represent Alma—the woman who saved my life spiritually when I was hospitalized at the age of eighteen (the full story is in my first book). When I waver in my faith or don't know how to pray, I just look at this quilt and remember that He has *all* things covered.

From the details to the cosmic, our Father loves us so much that He sacrificed Himself and conquered death that had separated us from Him. Understanding this kind of love is critical to our very being and purpose. I asked my friend, Pastor Ben Poole to write about it from his perspective as a dad.

One of the greatest moments was the birth of my first child, Aiden. I was excited to meet this baby that had been kicking me, responding to the sound of my voice, and causing his mother to grow exponentially. I knew love. Or I knew types of love. I knew about the love a child receives from his mother. I knew about the love a husband receives from and gives to his wife. I understood the love that came from family and friends. When I was nervously pacing the delivery room, I thought I knew what it would be like to hold my child - I knew nothing. When that baby boy was in my arms for the first time . . . well, I can't express the feeling in words. I had a new love. A love for a human being that I helped create. This was my son! I wanted to hold him tightly to my chest and simultaneously have a Lion King, Mufasa moment. I didn't just cry. I changed. I grew up in that moment. With my first child, I entered a new understanding of the universe.

I get to raise this miracle of life. I get to see the first steps and hear his squeaky voice when he becomes a pre-teen. I get to be a father, a dad. And it was going to be amazing and slightly terrifying. As Aiden looked wide-eyed throughout the room in those first few moments, my worldview changed forever. Fair warning, I am a follower of Jesus Christ. And I have always believed that He loves everyone. But now I know it.

I had been yanked to a new perspective. Through the birth of my child, I felt a small splinter of the Love that God the Father has for his sons and daughters. Perhaps you're reading this sarcastically and thinking "great for you." Maybe you never knew your father. It could be that you wish you had never known him. Fathers have an incredible responsibility to shape the way we view the world around us. Many dads never live up to that challenge. I don't know anything about your relationship with your dad. But here is what I do know. God has promised to be a Dad to the fatherless. In fact, it's in the Bible. Psalm 68:5-6 (NLT): "Father to the fatherless, defender of widows"—this is God, whose dwelling is holy. God places the lonely in families; he sets the prisoners free and gives them joy.

The Bible says that God is love. It's one of those things you hear and then say, "Sure, of course." But you can experience it. Maybe you already have. You may have had an experience of love and elation that pushes past what you thought was humanly possible. Your world got brighter, bigger, and full of mysterious love. I believe that God gave us His greatest ability. The ability to love and be loved. I have five children now, four boys and one girl. I'm thankful that I get to be their dad. It's not always easy. Yet it's always worth it. If we are created by a loving God, perhaps it's all worth it for him as well. Here is what I do know: love gives hope. Where there is love, there will always be hope! And if God himself says "I am love," then He loves you. How does God show His love? While we were still estranged and far from God, He sent His Son Jesus Christ to rescue us and show us a better way. Jesus was the One-man rescue team that paid the penalty for every mistake, stumble, and evil thing we have ever done.

God, in His mercy, made a way to bring us back into His family. Have you ever felt panic when you look up and realize you're missing your child? It's happened to me. He was just here. Where did he go? Your heart pounds so loudly you can hear it, and you began yelling out his or her name.

God is calling your name. Not only did He call your name, but He also sent a search and rescue team to find you. Are you found? It's possible God may have found you, but you haven't accepted rescue. Maybe you aren't sure about all of this. Here is a prayer that I have prayed several times. "God, I want to believe and help my unbelief. Jesus, if You're real, please rescue me. Give me Your hope and show me Your love." Once you begin to establish that belief, you're ready to accept rescue. You're ready to accept forgiveness and love, no matter what you have done. Our greatest struggle is internal: the question of "Am I worthy of love?"

If everyone knew everything about me, could anyone love me? Paul, who hated Jesus and had previously murdered Christians, said it this way. "God showed his great love for us by sending Christ to die for us while we were still sinners" (Romans 5:8 NLT). If a person who arrested, imprisoned, and participated in the murder of God's followers can be forgiven and loved by God, then so can you. In John 3:16 (NLT), Jesus Christ himself says that He loves you. "For this is how God loved the world: He gave his one and only Son so that everyone who believes in him will not perish but have eternal life."

If you are ready to receive that love and reject the guilt of your mistakes, please pray this prayer with all your heart, mind, soul, and strength: "God, I know I'm not perfect. I have messed up. I have hurt others, and I have done wrong. Please forgive me. Take away the burden of guilt. I believe that Jesus came to rescue me. I believe He died to save me and forgive my sins. I believe that He was nailed to a cross, died, buried, and returned to life. I believe Jesus has the power to give eternal life. I want to make Jesus my Savior and Lord starting now and throughout eternity." If you prayed that prayer with sincerity, then this is what the Bible says in Romans 10:9 (AMP "...if you acknowledge and confess with your mouth that Jesus is Lord [recognizing His power, authority, and majesty as God],and believe in your heart that God raised Him from the dead, you will be saved."

Come. Being saved or rescued is to know the love of God and respond to it. Love has victory against the power of sin and death in our lives and the world. Love aligns us in resistance to the spiritual forces actively trying to drag as many as possible into the darkness. Love is in the process of redeeming creation back to Himself, and we have a part to play.

Having faith and living faithfully doesn't take great intellect or eloquence as defined by society. I had the opportunity to share the gospel message with a group of teens with special needs. I began speaking about why Jesus went to the cross and experienced the crucifixion.

One of the young men with Down syndrome, named B.J., raised his hand and proclaimed, "Colleen, Jesus died for me— He shed His blood for me." The expression on his face told it all, and it was obvious he had just understood the unconditional gift of love that was given to him. All the youth leaders had tears in their eyes as we had just witnessed a miracle, the best kind of miracle: the beauty of accepting Christ as his Savior.

Later that afternoon, I saw B.J. preaching to his peers. I didn't comprehend everything he was saying, but I witnessed the youth around him. It was undeniable that they understood his message of love and hope. He was sharing the gospel message, and they were receiving it. He didn't use a large vocabulary, and no bright lights appeared—just the simple truth about the love of God for us and what our response should be.

How do I know God's love? I wouldn't be here without it. The fact that I wake up in the morning is an example of His priceless love for me. You can't put a cost on Him dying on the cross because it was the ultimate sacrifice. He was willing to suffer because He knew it would set us free to follow His example and love others.

"The LORD your God is with you, the Mighty
Warrior who saves. He will take great delight in you;
in his love he will no longer rebuke you, but will rejoice
over you with singing." (Zephaniah 3:17 NIV)

CHAPTER 9

LOVE ANNIHILATES EVIL

I always feel like I'm on a deadline, and I must finish certain tasks in this life. Yet this life is just a brief time—a "dash." "Well, that's depressing," you might be thinking. But it's not if you believe in eternity. This time on earth is the obstacle course that prepares us for the next journey. Sometimes we jump over hurdles, lizard-crawl under barbed wire, or need to be pulled up over a wall by our fellow participants. There are times we sprint, times we jump, and moments we need to be lifted off our knees and carried. We are being prepped to reach the goal line that will signal the beginning of the rest of our incredible journey.

It's so easy to get caught up in worldly circumstances, but we are really in a spiritual world and are part of a much bigger plan for which we each have a uniquely important role. Our prayers actually impact both present and future events. We are part of a spiritual battle but Christ has already secured the victory. Yes, this is sometimes hard to comprehend and even surreal. Yet, we are God's creations who are made to fight the good fight in love!

I was just listening to Louis Armstrong talk on YouTube before he sang, "What a Wonderful World,"[1] and he said the way to change this world is *love*! What's so cool is that when you fight evil with *love*, it has a ripple effect not only on earth but into eternity. God made this awesome plan for each of us. If we align our lives with His will, we will experience amazing moments, not just here but for eternity!

> So we're not giving up. How could we! Even though on the outside it often looks like things are falling apart on us, on the inside, where God is making new life, not a day goes by without his unfolding grace. These hard times are small potatoes compared to the coming good times, the lavish celebration prepared for us. There's far more here than meets the eye. The things we see now are here today, gone tomorrow. But the things we can't see now will last forever. (2 Corinthians 4:17 MSG)
>
> For our light affliction, which is but for a moment, works for us a far more exceeding and eternal weight of glory. (2 Corinthians 4:17 KJV)

A few years ago, I made a journal entry that exemplified the dichotomy between love and evil. I had to decide, once again, what action to take.

Not the adventure I was hoping for from a beautiful seaside town in middle California. Jim was training firefighters at the fire station, and I had to check out of the hotel. So, why not take a walk around town to look at the shops? Well, I should have known. A fight broke out in front of me between two men who were homeless. The younger man was shirtless, displaying gang language tattooed to his back, which I recognized from my work as a therapist on "suicide row" in the Illinois Youth Center and from having done ministry in gang territories. I also recognized signs of delusional schizophrenia from the older man—the one whose head was being bashed repeatedly into the sidewalk. I won't go into all the details, but it took a while for the police to come. So hard. After that, I decided to wait in the coffee shop near the fire station. On the way, while waiting for the crosswalk signal, a youth strolled up and nodded his head in my direction. He then proceeded to lift the edge of his shirt, showing his friend and I the gun he had stuffed into the waistband of his pants. I returned in the direction I had come to get the police, but the two young men disappeared around the corner and were gone. I didn't want to disturb Jim's training, so I sat at the coffee shop. I have traveled to many beautiful places and, unfortunately, have witnessed this kind of stuff in several of those locations. It's also existed in every town I've lived in since I can remember.

The dichotomy of life. The realization that things need to change. So much anger, pain, loneliness, etc. The other day, I saw a guy in his twenties with a sign that said he was willing to subject himself to significant verbal abuse if you gave him money. Usually, I give food or bottled water, but I gave him a dollar (and yeah, maybe he used it for alcohol or drugs). I told him I didn't want to verbally abuse him.

"Go ahead, if you want. Everyone else does. I can handle it."

"No one deserves to be abused for any amount of money. You have a purpose, and you are important," I replied.

He was so shocked. I wish kind words didn't shock him. I don't have the big-picture solutions. I do know that people need to know love. No easy answers. I prayed, as I do every day, "God put me where you want me."

I see things that aren't beautiful, but I never want to turn my head away from the hurts and evil. I don't want to be silent. We can't save the world, but we can touch one another's lives. One person at a time. I am far from perfect and make tons of mistakes, but there are always opportunities to make things a little better while I am still here on earth. This is what real life is about, and I'm thankful for the blessings that do exist. And there are many.

There was a very special moment in my life when love touched me. I recall a guy being compassionate toward me as I was bullied in sixth grade. A hairdresser had tried to thin out my naturally curly hair, but it was a mess (we didn't have gel in those days). I was underweight and sounded like Darth Vader most of the time (severe asthma), and I had a pale face with bluish lips (heart stuff). Although I tried to be "cool" with the wide-tooth, multi-colored comb in my back pocket and a black t-shirt with rainbow glitter that said "Disco Queen" on it, the look just wasn't working.

I was at the roller rink, and it was a girls' skate, which meant girls had to ask the guys to skate. As I went through the line, the boys called me "ugly dog" and other names. I was so humiliated that I just wanted to disappear. Then one of the older guys that knew our family came up to me and took my hands to skate. I was so nervous that I couldn't explain how I positioned my arms, but it was awkward. The other guys were snickering, but they stopped when he gave them a look. He was considered one of the "good-looking/popular" guys and had a heart of gold. I will never forget that kind gesture! We never know what impact we will have if we are kind to others.

Luke 6:27 (NIV) states, "But to you who are listening I say: Love your enemies, do good to those who hate you . . ." Not easy at all. It's easy to "spread the love" to kind people. But what about those who aren't so nice? How can we love them? Do we have to like them? First of all, we need to recognize that God is love. We can't love without His love. We are made in His image and therefore, have the capacity to love. If we force it or will it to happen, it won't happen.

Working in the Illinois Youth Center taught me a great deal about loving others. These youth committed hideous crimes and were incarcerated for a reason. I won't go into detail because I wrote about my experience in my first book. These young men are no different from you and me. Earlier, I said I don't condone their crimes. However, learning of their past made me realize if I had been raised in the same environment, I may have easily committed the crimes they did. They had no perspective of right from wrong. They had all been severely, emotionally, and physically abused.

One of the inmates asked me about Mariah Carey's song "Hero." "Do you think anyone would ever see me as being good? Or as their hero?"

"I do," I said.

From that moment on, his personality changed. He started to become a positive person with hope and goals. He needed love. He needed to know his value. We all do. Sometimes, it's easier to love strangers than people we know who have hurt us. I get this! Matthew 6:14-15 (NIV) says, "For if you forgive other people when they sin against you, your heavenly Father will also forgive you. But if you do not forgive others their sins, your Father will not forgive your sins."

Easier said than done. I love Lysa TerKeurst's Bible study, *Forgiving What You Can't Forget.* I'm working on it now, as I want to love people with nothing hindering me because that's an act of love to our God! She wrote, "My ability to forgive others rises and falls on leaning into what Jesus has already done, which allows His grace for me to flow freely through me (Ephesians 4:7). Forgiveness isn't an act of my determination. Forgiveness is only made possible by my cooperation."[2]

I am not going to go deep into the subject of forgiveness, but usually, it's critical in loving those we know who hurt us. This doesn't mean we can't have healthy boundaries if needed, but it does mean having an attitude of loving others as God loves us (John 15:12).

I want to add that people who have been hurt usually hurt others. It's hard to recognize their hurt when they are inflicting it on you. Sometimes, we need to pause and acknowledge this fact before responding to their words or behavior. In addition, we may disagree with someone's thoughts and beliefs, and conflict can occur. Yet, there are reasons people are passionate about what they believe. Sometimes, love is really listening to the other person and understanding where he or she is coming from. It doesn't mean compromising your beliefs, but it does mean that you have the opportunity to listen to and pray for that person. Prayer is the ultimate love language and can break down barriers that exist.

Endnotes

1   RoundMidnightTV. 2011. "Louis Armstrong - What a Wonderful World (Original Spoken Intro Version) ABC Records 1967, 1970." *YouTube*. https://www.youtube.com/watch?v=2nGKqH26xlg.

2   Lysa TerKeurst, *Forgiving What You Can't Forget: Discover How to Move On, Make Peace with Painful Memories, and Create a Life That's Beautiful Again* (Thomas Nelson, 2020), 7.

CHAPTER 10

ENCOURAGEMENT

Christianity is not just involved with "salvation," but with the total man in the total world. The Christian message begins with the existence of God forever, and then with creation. It does not begin with salvation. We must be thankful for salvation, but the Christian message is more than that. Man has a value because he is made in the image of God.[1] –Francis Schaeffer

Chapter 1 in this book starts with encouragement to embrace the truth that you are not here by accident and, without a doubt, have a unique purpose for this specific time in history. You then read how critical community is to the fulfillment of your purpose. That, as the body of Christ, we must engage in fellowship with others who are on the same path as described in 2 Timothy 1:9 (NKJV): ". . . who saved us, and called us with a holy calling, not according to our works, but according to his own purpose and grace, which was given us in Christ Jesus before times eternal." There is an interdependency intended for us.

Chapters 3 and following describe God's love, gifts, and the tools He gives us as His children, which help us navigate these times. Now, it's time to be encouraged to *continue* the mission we are called to individually and collectively. Before doing so, I would like you to embrace these verses as God's promises! These are critical tools for the battle we are presently facing.

"I know that You can do all things, And that no thought or purpose of Yours can be restrained." (Job 42:2 AMP)

"'No weapon formed against you shall prosper, And every tongue which rises against you in judgment, You shall condemn. This is the heritage of the servants of the Lord, and their righteousness is from Me,' Says the Lord." (Isaiah 54:17 NKJV)

For the gifts and the calling of God are irrevocable [for He does not withdraw what He has given, nor does He change His mind about those to whom He gives His grace or to whom He sends His call]. (Romans 11:29 AMP)

With this in mind, we constantly pray for you, that our God may make you worthy of his calling, and that by his power he may bring to fruition your every desire for goodness and your every deed prompted by faith. We pray this so that the name of our Lord Jesus may be glorified in you, and you in him, according to the grace of our God and the Lord Jesus Christ. (2 Thessalonians 1:11-12 NIV)

Of note, in the above verses, you'll find a few keywords: "for goodness" and "prompted by faith." In the desire for fellowship, we typically align ourselves with others who interpret scriptures similarly. Care must be taken here because, more recently, some people have ignored certain scriptures in favor of others, resulting in a very lopsided belief system. Ignoring words like "desiring goodness" and "prompted by faith" alters the meaning of 2 Thessalonians 1:11-12 to suggest that every Christian has the right to have God fulfill his or her every desire and need. Ignoring those words also de-emphasizes verses like, "Consider it pure joy, my brothers and sisters, whenever you face trials of many kinds . . ." (James 1:2 NIV), and Romans 8:18 talks about that glory that is revealed in us through suffering. In Ephesians 6, the apostle Paul says our struggles are not against flesh and blood but against spiritual powers.

God uses trials, suffering, and struggles to refine us. He strengthens us as we rely on Him. Be careful of the popular health and wealth, name it and claim it, or decree and declare doctrines. They say if you just have enough faith or pray the right formula, you will be rich or healthy, "lacking for nothing!" Under scrutiny, this is the message of the false prophets.

I'm going to pause here because this is very critical at this point in our history as we see false teachers and prophets growing in numbers. Don't get me wrong, God can and still does perform miracles, which was discussed in Chapter 3 on "Unanswered Prayers." Yet, false teachers of the Word twist the scriptures. I've even heard them saying they are "God's anointed" and should not be physically touched or verbally challenged. They "prophesy" visions that don't come true. What does the Word say about this?

For the time will come when people will not put up with sound doctrine. Instead, to suit their desires, they will gather around them a great number of teachers to say what their itching ears want to hear. They will turn their ears away from the truth and turn aside to myths. (2 Timothy 4:3-4 NIV)

Dear friends, do not believe every spirit, but test the spirits to see whether they are from God, because many false prophets have gone out into the world. This is how you can recognize the Spirit of God: Every spirit that acknowledges that Jesus Christ has come in the flesh is from God, but every spirit that does not acknowledge Jesus is not from God. This is the spirit of the antichrist, which you have heard is coming and even now is already in the world. You, dear children, are from God and have overcome them, because the one who is in you is greater than the one who is in the world. They are from the world and therefore speak from the viewpoint of the world, and the world listens to them. We are from God, and whoever knows God listens to us; but whoever is not from God does not listen to us. This is how we recognize the Spirit of truth and the spirit of falsehood. (1 John 4:1-6 NIV)

But there were also false prophets among the people, just as there will be false teachers among you. They will secretly introduce destructive heresies, even denying the sovereign Lord who bought them—bringing swift destruction on themselves. Many will follow their depraved conduct and will bring the way of truth into disrepute. In their greed these teachers will exploit you with fabricated stories. Their condemnation has long been hanging over them, and their destruction has not been sleeping. For if God did not spare angels when they sinned, but sent them to hell, putting them in chains of darkness to be held for judgment . . ." (2 Peter 2:1-4a NIV)

There are more scriptures on false prophets and teachers, but you get the picture. God intends for us to be made worthy of His calling, namely, to bring forth goodness and be prompted by faith. These things do not always get a personal reward. However, they promote the Kingdom of God here on Earth as we participate in God's greater plan. When in doubt of how to act during a situation or trial, remember 1 Thessalonians 5:16-18 (ESV): "Rejoice always, pray without ceasing, give thanks in all circumstances, for this is the will of God in Christ Jesus for you." Such as it was with true heroes of the faith, among whom Corrie ten Boom and Dietrich Bonhoeffer must be included. They both took a significant personal risk to save others' lives. During World War II, they took action while whole churches justified inaction and sang louder to drown out the sound of the trains carrying innocent men, women, and children to their deaths. *Sing a Little Louder²* is a moving short film based on one man's recounting.

Corrie ten Boom was a Christian woman whose family helped hundreds of Jews escape the Nazi Holocaust in the Netherlands during World War II. After being betrayed by an informer, she and ten of her family members were eventually imprisoned in the concentration camps, where she was one of the only survivors. The book and movie *The Hiding Place³* are based on those real-life events and tell the story of their "underground railroad" to save Jews and others being persecuted. God blessed their desire for goodness and their deeds prompted by faith, but it cost them dearly. Ten Boom related that her sister, Betsie, was thankful for fleas in their barracks and how God was glorified in that. In the movie sequel *Return to The Hiding Place⁴*, two young men ask a board of pastors how they can stand by and do nothing, telling them, "Your Christianity makes the Gestapo look gracious."

I have used scripture throughout this book to show that these writings are just as relevant today as they were 2,000 years ago. Corrie ten Boom believed in the Bible and God as its inspiration. She stated, "When a train goes through a tunnel, and it gets dark, you don't throw away the ticket and jump off. You sit still and trust the Engineer."[5] Corrie lived by her faith and chose to speak and act out of love for Him so He could be glorified through her. She said of the Bible, "The truth is that God's viewpoint is sometimes different from ours—so different that we could not even guess at it unless He had given us a Book that tells us such things."[6]

Bonhoeffer was another Christian who stood up to Hitler's schemes and fought against the Nazis' plans. Through him, even the Nazis witnessed the true love of Christ. Bonhoeffer has a remarkable story shared in his biography: *Bonhoeffer: Pastor, Martyr, Prophet, Spy,*[7] written by Eric Metaxas. The title explains that we would find out that Bonhoeffer would be murdered for what he did as he stayed loyal to God's goodness.

"On April 9, 1945, Lutheran pastor and theologian Dietrich Bonhoeffer was hanged at Flossenburg, only days before the American liberation of that POW camp. The last words of the brilliant and courageous 39-year-old opponent of Nazism were, 'This is the end—for me, the beginning of life.'"[8]

In his book, *Hitler's Cross*[9], Dr. Erwin Lutzer explains that as Bonhoeffer was escorted to his death, a Nazi physician was amazed at how peaceful this man was. We know that only a loving God can provide "peace that surpasses understanding." We may question why God did not save him, but God's ways are mysterious, and the death of this martyr would impact thousands for generations to come. Bonhoeffer lived out the verse, "Greater love has no one than this: to lay down one's life for one's friends" (John 15:13 NIV). He understood God's purpose for him and followed his calling. God was glorified as this faithful servant's unselfish actions expanded His kingdom on earth. May we have the courage to follow that example.

Bonhoeffer considered the Bible "God's Word" as he wrote in his book, *Life Together: The Classic Exploration of Christian Community*: "The first service one owes to others in a community involves listening to them. Just as our love for God begins with listening to God's Word, the beginning of love for others is learning to listen to them. God's love for us is shown by the fact that God gives God's Word and lends us God's ear. We do God's work for our brothers and sisters when we learn to listen to them."[10]

In contrast, I often wondered how some Christians were apathetic to Hitler's horrific and twisted evil toward the Jews and anyone they deemed unworthy of living. Their theologies and philosophies opposed the very Word of God. After all,

Jesus was Jewish and a Middle Easterner (Luke 4:14-30). God clearly states in His Word that *all* people are made in *His* image (Genesis 1:27). He also gave us free will. We can choose to either accept His work of redemption on our behalf and reflect His light by desiring goodness and doing deeds prompted by faith, or we can reject it. By default, that rejection ties us to the kingdom of darkness and the "rulers of the darkness of this age" (Ephesians 6:2). As Jesus said in Matthew 12:30 (NIV), "Whoever is not with me is against me, and whoever does not gather with me scatters."

We also see in God's Word, again and again, an overarching theme of His love and desire for redemption of His creation. Going back to Chapter 1, we are created in His image. Therefore, isn't it just like the enemy to wreak havoc on all God's creation? Hitler ignored the value of human life. He chose to annihilate Jews even though he was part Jewish himself and had been bullied for it in his youth. This is further discussed in the video "Who was Hitler's Grandfather? Why Should You Care?"[11] In the video, Dr. Sax explains what influenced Hitler's mind and eventually his blatantly evil actions.

Bitterness (keyword) twisted his heart, and he succumbed to occultism and the occult who prey on those who feel alone or rejected (critical point). He and his Reich used propaganda and ethnic Nationalism to divide the people of Germany. "Divide and conquer" is a popular method of manipulation in warfare. His influence was pure evil, and he promoted his ethnic cleansing and eugenics agenda to an economically and morally weakened nation.

While it's historically debatable whether Margaret Sanger, founder of Planned Parenthood, was a racist, it is known in her writings that she was a proponent of eugenics. Eugenics is "the practice or advocacy of controlled selective breeding of human populations (as by sterilization) to improve the population's genetic composition."[12] She was very blunt about the concept. In her book, *The Pivot of Civilization*, Sanger wrote, "Every feeble-minded girl or woman of the hereditary type, especially of the moron class should be segregated during the reproductive period."[13] Sadly, some other Americans agreed, and you can read a horrific history of forced sterilization with estimates between 70,000 to possibly 150,000 victims at that time.

In the case, Buck v. Bell, 274 U.S. 200 (1927), is a decision of the United States Supreme Court, written by Justice Oliver Wendell Holmes, Jr., in which the Court ruled that a state statute permitting compulsory sterilization of the unfit, including the intellectually disabled, "for the protection and health of the state" did not violate the Due Process Clause of the Fourteenth Amendment to the United States Constitution.[14]

An unbelievable fact is that Buck vs. Bell has never been overturned. The last documented forced sterilization occurred in 1981.[15] This does not negate the possibility that more undocumented forced sterilizations have occurred. In addition, in September 2017, APA News in Kenya reported the following:

> That at least 500,000 young girls and women may be infertile, following a tetanus vaccine administered by the government in 2014 and 2015: "Hundreds of thousands of our girls and women, aged between 14 and 49, from the fastest growing populations in the country will not have children, because of the state-sponsored sterilization that was sold to the country as tetanus vaccination," Odinga declared.[16]

As we see, Hitler did adopt much of the concept of American eugenics. "Hitler studied American eugenics laws. He tried to legitimize his anti-Semitism by medicalizing it and wrapping it in the more palatable pseudoscientific facade of eugenics."[17]

Why is this all critical to discuss at this time in history? I've been studying the Holocaust for over thirty-five years. I see that it was not just a methodically thought-out psychological battle but also (and mainly) a spiritual one. I've seen the communist aftermath in Eastern Europe. I've met with several Holocaust survivors at Auschwitz and here in the United States. I've spoken to a congregation in Poland that ministers to Holocaust survivors and have looked out the same windows as Anne Frank onto the streets of Amsterdam. I have felt dark spiritual oppression. This oppression was spread as Hitler slowly manipulated and brainwashed people with his agenda. It was not something that happened overnight. Many realized too late that Hitler was not "desiring good" in a Godly sense but was, instead, opposed to Christianity.

"In Hitler's eyes, Christianity was a religion fit only for slaves," wrote Alan Bullock, "Its teaching, he declared, was a rebellion against the natural law of selection by struggle of the fittest."[18] We know "survival of the fittest" is a coined term related to Darwinism. Going back to the fact that "both social Darwinists and eugenicists proposed eugenic solutions in dealing with the 'unfit' and the 'unworthy,' both called for involuntary sexual sterilization and segregation of the mentally ill, the feebleminded, the poor, immigrants, etc."[19] Now reread these scriptures that were quoted in chapter 1 that contradict the beliefs of Darwin, Sanger, and Hitler.

For you created my inmost being; you knit me together in my mother's womb. I praise you because I am fearfully and wonderfully made; your works are wonderful, I know that full well. My frame was not hidden from you when I was made in the secret place, when I was woven together in the depths of the earth. Your eyes saw my unformed body; all the days ordained for me were written in your book before one of them came to be. (Psalm 139:13-16 NIV)

As a church, we need to realize that history repeats itself. We need to recognize evil in all its subtleties, and we need to fight it. How do we fight evil?

1) Again, recognize that we are all made in God's image, and we all have a purpose (Chapter 1). "So God created man in His own image, in the image of God he created him; male and female he created them" (Genesis 1:27 ESV). Also, check out Acts 10:34-35 (NIV): "Then Peter began to speak: 'I now realize how true it is that God does not show favoritism but accepts from every nation the one who fears him and does what is right." And then these two important verses:

For the LORD your God is God of gods and Lord of lords, the great God, mighty and awesome, who shows no partiality and accepts no bribes. He defends the cause of the fatherless and the widow, and loves the foreigner residing among you, giving them food and clothing. And you are to love those who are foreigners, for you yourselves were foreigners in Egypt. (Deuteronomy 10:17-19 NIV)

We know we were created for a purpose, and we are not just fighting physical or psychological battles but spiritual ones (Ephesians 6), as we saw in Chapter 5. The Bible clearly states the battle we are fighting: "a great multitude that no one could number, from every nation, from all tribes and peoples and languages, standing before the throne and before the Lamb" (Revelation 7:9-10 ESV).

2) As mentioned in Chapter 9, believe that love triumphs over evil. God has a lot to say about ministering to our enemies. "Do not be overcome by evil, but overcome evil with good" (Romans 12:21 NIV).

3) Be discerning of what you are being fed in the media. Just because it's a law or in the news, that doesn't make it right. We need to ask: "Does it align with God's Word?"

Finally, brothers and sisters, whatever is true, whatever is noble, whatever is right, whatever is pure, whatever is lovely, whatever is admirable—if anything is excellent or praiseworthy—think about such things. (Philippians 4:8 NIV)

Let no one deceive you with empty words, for because of these things the wrath of God comes upon the sons of disobedience. Therefore do not become partners with them; for at one time you were darkness, but now you are light in the Lord. Walk as children of light (for the fruit of light is found in all that is good and right and true), and try to discern what is pleasing to the Lord. (Ephesians 5:6-10 ESV)

4) Consider the cost and decide to act like our brothers and sisters have in other countries. We are starting to feel more pressure to conform. Good will be called evil, and evil will be called good (Isaiah 5:20-21, Romans 1:18-23).

We must see ourselves as warriors for Christ. There are some crazy battles out there, but victory is His. I was just with dear sisters in Christ from India and Germany via video chat today. They are amazing women I've met through different experiences in my life. They shared what's happening within their countries. Interesting things are happening all over the world due to the Covid Pandemic and other trials. Yesterday, I was connected with national leaders and those leading the fight against sex trafficking. From international to very personal, the list of prayer requests gets longer and longer. It can be overwhelming!

So, is there hope? I believe so. Sometimes it feels like the enemy's army is large, but God uses single people or small armies to overcome impossible situations, and in doing so, He shows His love for us.

Remember the story of Esther that illustrates this point. Esther, an orphan, fasted and prayed and went before the king. Haman (a bad dude), who wanted to annihilate the Jews, was exposed. Through Esther's courage and faithfulness, the Jews were saved (Esther 5)! David, a shepherd boy, killed Goliath (1 Samuel 17). Joshua and his army blew the trumpets, and the walls of Jericho came down (Joshua 6:1-27). Jehoshaphat's army had three armies against them, but Jehoshaphat was told to worship, and the enemies turned on each other (2 Chronicles 20). Daniel prayed three times a day, and Nebuchadnezzar wasn't keen on it at all. Daniel, long story short, was not only spared but became royalty. Nebuchadnezzar was like Hitler. God humbled Nebuchadnezzar's heart, and he turned to God (Daniel 4:25-35). Gideon, a humble underdog with only 300 men/soldiers, had the enemy delivered into their hands by God (Judges 7).

There are so many more stories, and they're not just stories. Archeological digs plus other historical documents confirm many biblical events. And the ultimate battle was won by Jesus' birth, life, crucifixion, and resurrection as ancient prophecies foretold! "Therefore the Lord himself shall give you a sign; Behold, a virgin shall conceive, and bear a son, and shall call his name Immanuel" (Isaiah 7:14 ESV). This was fulfilled by Jesus' birth and recorded in (Matthew 1:18-23).

Because Jesus came to us and did what we could not do for ourselves, we can fight the battle because "God is with us!" We are not alone. It can look like we're losing, but God will be glorified! So, you are not defeated. Nothing can separate you from God's love (Romans 8:37-39 NIV).

No, in all these things, we are more than conquerors through him who loved us. For I am convinced that neither death nor life, neither angels nor demons, neither the present nor the future, nor any powers, neither height nor depth, nor anything else in all creation, will be able to separate us from the love of God that is in Christ Jesus our Lord.

Here's the deal in short. Jesus encouraged us, "I have told you these things, so that in me you may have peace. In this world you will have trouble. But take heart! I have overcome the world" (John 16:33 NIV). He walked before us, and He walks with us. Again, read Ephesians 6:10-20, and you will see the tools we need to persevere through the battle.

Encouragement

Endnotes

1 Francis A. Schaeffer, *Art & the Bible* (IVP Books 2009), 89.

2 https://singloudermovie.com/.

3 Ann Chegwidden, *The Hiding Place* movie, directed by James Collier, United States: World Wide Pictures.

4 Peter C. Spencer, Josiah Spencer, Bart Gavigan, John Rhys-Davies, Mimi Sagadin, and Craig Robert Young, *Return to the Hiding Place*, https://www.imdb.com/title/tt1691153/.

5 https://www.brainyquote.com/quotes/corrie_ten_boom_393675.

6 Corrie ten Boom, *The Hiding Place* (Chosen Books 1971; Bantam Books 1974), 160.

7 Eric Metaxas, *Bonhoeffer: Pastor, Martyr, Prophet, Spy* (Thomas Nelson Pub. 2020).

8 "Anti-Nazi theologian Dietrich Bonhoeffer is hanged," https://www.history.com/this-day-in-history/defiant-theologian-dietrich-bonhoeffer-is-hanged.

9 Erwin W. Lutzer, *Hitler's Cross* (Chicago: Moody Press 1995).

10 Dietrich Bonhoeffer, *Life Together: The Classic Exploration of Christian Community* (HarperOne 2015), 75-76.

11 Leonard Sax MD, PhD, *Who was Hitler's grandfather? Why should you care?* (2019), https://www.leonardsax.com/Who-Was-Hitlers-Grandfather-Why-Should-You-Care/.

12 https://www.merriam-webster.com/dictionary/eugenics.

13 Margaret Sanger, H. G. Wells, and American Birth Control League, *The Pivot of Civilization* (Queens Ny: Streetlib 2018).

14 "Buck v. Bell: Case Summary and Case Brief," February 12, 2019, https://legaldictionary.net/buck-v-bell/.

15 "Forced Sterilizations in the U.S.," August 9, 2021, https://www.thoughtco.com/forced-sterilization-in-united-states-721308.

16 "Mass sterilization of millions of African girls through tetanus vaccine scandal broadens as Kenyan laboratory attacked," https://nexusnewsfeed.com/article/human-rights/mass-sterilization-of-millions-of-african-girls-through-tetanus-vaccine-scandal-broadens-as-kenyan-laboratory-attacked/.

17 Edwin Black, "The Horrifying American Roots of Nazi Eugenics," September 2003, https://historynewsnetwork.org/article/1796.

18 Alan Bullock, *Hitler: A Study in Tyranny* (Harper Perennial 1962, abridged edition), 219.

19 E. Kurbegovic, "Social Darwinism," April 29, 2014, http://eugenicsarchive.ca/Discover/Tree/535eee377095aa0000000259.

CHAPTER 11

BETTER THAN A FAIRYTALE ENDING

Before we get to the unbelievably fantastic ending, let's go even a little bit deeper.

Take a deep breath. Persecution. Ouch! Not a fun topic at all. But let's start with a beautiful and encouraging passage from God's Word/His Promise!

> "Blessed are those who are persecuted for righteousness' sake, for theirs is the kingdom of Heaven. Blessed are you when others revile you and persecute you and utter all kinds of evil against you falsely on my account. Rejoice and be glad, for your reward is great in Heaven, for so they persecuted the prophets who were before you." (Matthew 5:10-12 ESV)

"Your reward is great in heaven" sounds so good, but what about the prerequisites required while we're here on earth? While we certainly enjoy happiness and crave immediate gratification, those desires are precisely the characteristics that false prophets and teachers exploit to stunt spiritual growth and disarm us for the coming battle. Paul encouraged the church in Rome to follow Abrahams's example. Abraham's faith was strong, "being fully persuaded that God had power to do what he had promised. This is why 'it was credited to him as righteousness'" (Romans 4:21-22 NIV). He encourages us too. Our faith is also credited to us as righteousness.

> but also for us, to whom God will credit righteousness—for us who believe in him who raised Jesus our Lord from the dead. He was delivered over to death for our sins and was raised to life for our justification. (Romans 4:24-25 NIV)

This gives us peace and a reason for hope. Paul says in Romans 5:1-2 (NIV):

> Therefore since we have been justified through faith, we have peace with God through our Lord Jesus Christ, through whom we have gained access by faith into this grace in which we now stand. And we boast in the hope of the glory of God.

People tend to boast about many things: wealth, self-sufficiency, looks, possessions, popularity, etc. Our ultimate boast should be "in the hope of the glory of God." This is what can sustain us in times of trial when all else will fail us. It keeps us from paralyzing fear and worry. Paul continues to encourage us to endure hardships to the end with the help of the Holy Spirit.

Not only so, but we also glory in our sufferings, because we know that suffering produces perseverance; perseverance, character; and character, hope. And hope does not put us to shame, because God's love has been poured out into our hearts through the Holy Spirit, who has been given to us. (Romans 5:3-5 NIV)

We must be wise in following the examples of the heroes of the faith. If we persevere with God's grace and strength, the outcome will be amazing. Let's look at 2 Corinthians 12:9-10 ESV:

But he said to me, "My grace is sufficient for you, for my power is made perfect in weakness." Therefore I will boast all the more gladly of my weaknesses, so that the power of Christ may rest upon me. For the sake of Christ, then, I am content with weaknesses, insults, hardships, persecutions, and calamities. For when I am weak, then I am strong.

I think of Christians in other countries. They have dealt not just with persecution but are being killed for their faith. As their church is being attacked, I've heard stories about our brothers and sisters singing praises to God with one hand reaching heaven and one hand on their throat, anticipating martyrdom. How? It's only by the peace that God's grace provides at the moment. Faith, strong and tested by trial, transcends this world and can only be given by God.

I have met and witnessed this kind of faith in survivors of the genocide in Rwanda. I strongly recommend that you watch the documentary called *Unforgivable*.[1]

> Unforgivable explores the relationship between Alice, a Tutsi woman who lost her child and her hand in the genocide against the Tutsi in 1994, and Emmanuel, the Hutu man who attacked her and her family. After serving his prison term, Emmanuel seeks out Alice and confesses to being the one who cut off her hand. Alice extends him forgiveness, and together, they run the Ukuri Kuganze Association, providing housing and counseling for genocide survivors and facilitating reconciliation between them and their former attackers.
>
> Only a good God can bring redemption out of something so evil.

If we, hypothetically, put ourselves in those situations, fear would be a natural reaction. Remember that God has probably already helped you through trials you could not have imagined yourself surviving. He was faithful to sustain you. If you haven't experienced that kind of deep trial yet, be prepared for the challenge and practice leaning on Him now, so you are not derailed when the time comes.

If you had a crystal ball and saw some of what the future held for you, you'd surely (or I know I would) say, "I won't be able to endure that." If someone said I would hold my daughter as she died, I would have told that person I would not survive. Yet, I did. Not by my strength but His. As His child, and belonging to His kingdom, fear not. He will give us all we need for anything we need to endure.

I understand how difficult these times are personally, nationally, and globally. Yet, I'd encourage you to embrace an eternal perspective, as I've mentioned earlier in this book. I want to bring us back to the Introduction where I mentioned how it is sometimes to get out of bed. We need to remember where and in whom our hope lies. This is what I wrote when I woke up the other morning.

My brain is going in multiple directions. One is to count my blessings—a practice I have learned helps get the day off to a positive start. Another is trying not to be anxious about all that's happening. It is tempting to look at the news, but I am choosing not to right now. I can't believe I'm going to say it, but I miss the days when the news would repeat the same story for weeks. In those times, events did not unfold at the pace they do these days. Now, I watch, and in five minutes, there is so much information that it's hard to process. There are so many directives to do this or don't do this for your health, money, family, country, etc. Are we even being fed the truth? Knowing what I know from other resources, we are not hearing the truth most of the time.

I miss the 1970s, '80s, '90s, and, well, February 2020, before life flipped us upside down. Don't get me wrong; my life hasn't been the easiest. I do consider myself blessed. Back then, we didn't have this looming, strange feeling about where we are going globally. Then I read this:

"You will hear of wars and rumors of wars, but see to it that you are not alarmed. Such things must happen, but the end is still to come. Nation will rise against nation and kingdom against kingdom. There will be famines and earthquakes in various places. All these are the beginning of birth pains.

"Then you will be handed over to be persecuted and put to death, and all nations will hate you because of me. At that time, many will turn away from the faith and will betray and hate each other, and many false prophets will appear and deceive many people. Because of the increase of wickedness, the love of most will grow cold, but the one who stands firm to the end will be saved." (Matthew 24:6-13 NIV)

There is hope.

While we may not be going through persecution unto death here, many of our brothers and sisters who live in other countries are.

If you read the Bible from beginning to end, you know three gardens are mentioned. I've studied them for years. In her book, *It's Not Supposed to Be This Way,*[2] Lysa TerKeurst does an excellent job of explaining the garden of Eden and the garden in Revelation. The title of her book alone is an excellent summary of what happened between those two gardens. I'm going to include the garden of Gethsemane.

We are introduced to a naked man and woman in the first garden and some crazy talking snake. This profound event describes the moment the world changed. We would have had this fantastic chilled-out place with unbelievable beauty, in which man and woman could walk in a close relationship with God. However, temptation happened, and despite my wanting to have a serious discussion with Eve about birthing pains (not cool), who knows what I would have done.

What if the fruit of that tree was chocolate? I can imagine that I might have resisted, but we know this is much deeper than eating the forbidden fruit. Seriously, Evil and Death entered the equation when Adam and Eve disobeyed God. Harsh reality. What was a close, intimate friendship with God changed to shame, hiding, and separation from Him.

Then there is the garden of Gethsemane, where Jesus prayed. "Going a little farther, he fell with his face to the ground and prayed, 'My Father, if it is possible, may this cup be taken from me. Yet not as I will, but as you will'" (Matthew 26:39 NIV). Intense. I will not compare my life to His, but I have also asked, "Can this time or trial pass completely or, at least, quickly?" I have been face down in despair at times. Then, I feel God's peace, grace, and strength (definitely not my own) and can say, "Your will God, not mine."

I'd love to tell you there are no struggles at times, but I have, like Jacob, wrestled with God. Yet, God is not the enemy, and I am not God. Remember the snake ("serpent" sounds eerier); we know who that represents. What's surreal is that Eve would bear children, and through that lineage would be born Jesus, who would be persecuted and put to death for our sake. He defeated death and lives to give us eternal life. Read that last sentence again because it's through His love for us that we share in this victory. *"Nothing* in all creation will ever be able to separate us from the love of God that is revealed in Christ Jesus our Lord," as promised in Romans 8:39 (NLT, emphasis added). And Luke 10:19-20 (NIV) states:

"I have given you authority to trample on snakes and scorpions and to overcome all the power of the enemy; nothing will harm you. However, do not rejoice that the spirits submit to you, but rejoice that your names are written in Heaven."

How amazing is this? *And* there are more awesome things to come. We will receive crowns in heaven, depending on our position in this life, and I encourage you to study more about them. I won't go into detail on each one, but here they are: 1) Crown of Righteousness (2 Timothy 4:8), 2) Incorruptible Crown (1 Corinthians 9:25), 3) Crown of Life (James 1:12), 4) Crown of Glory (1 Peter 5:2-4), and 5) Crown of Rejoicing (1 Thessalonians 2:19).

1 Peter 1:3-4 (ESV) exclaims:

Blessed be the God and Father of our Lord Jesus Christ! According to his great mercy, he has caused us to be born again to a living hope through the resurrection of Jesus Christ from the dead, to an inheritance that is imperishable, undefiled, and unfading, kept in heaven for you.

Remember that we know how the Good Book ends: "happily ever after" for those who have been restored by God, redeemed by Christ, and rest in Him. You are loved; you are here for a grand purpose. You are valued, and make a difference as God, the Creator, has chosen you for His own and adopted you into His Kingdom! To God be the glory! These Truths should help you to have a "good morning!"

...the twenty-four elders fall down before him who sits on the throne and worship him who lives for ever and ever. They lay their crowns before the throne and say: "You are worthy, our Lord and God, to receive glory and honor and power, for you created all things, and by your will, they were created and have their being." (Revelation 4:10-11 NIV)

And God shall wipe away all tears from their eyes; and there shall be no more death, neither sorrow, nor crying, neither shall there be any more pain: for the former things are passed away. (Revelation 21:4 KJV)

Eden will be restored.

Then the angel showed me the river of the water of life, as clear as crystal, flowing from the throne of God and of the Lamb down the middle of the great street of the city. On each side of the river stood the tree of life, bearing twelve crops of fruit, yielding its fruit every month. And the leaves of the tree are for the healing of the nations. No longer will there be any curse. The throne of God and of the Lamb will be in the city, and his servants will serve him. (Revelation 22:1-3 NIV)

And here's what the final chapter of the Bible promises.

"Look, I am coming soon! My reward is with me, and I will give to each person according to what they have done. I am the Alpha and the Omega, the First and the Last, the Beginning and the End." (Revelation 22:12-13 NIV)

Our response to all this can only be:

Day and night they never stop saying: "Holy, holy, holy is the Lord God Almighty, who was, and is, and is to come." . . . "You are worthy, our Lord and God, to receive glory and honor and power, for you created all things, and by your will they were created and have their being." (Revelation 4:8-11 NIV)

As the apostle Paul wrote:

I eagerly expect and hope that I will in no way be ashamed, but will have sufficient courage so that now as always Christ will be exalted in my body, whether by life or by death.(Philippians 1:20-21 NIV)

This may be the end of the book, but it's the beginning and maybe a defining moment for you to continue to draw closer to Christ, grow in faith and faithfulness, and persist until you are face to face with Him.

"Holy, holy, holy is the LORD Almighty; the whole earth is full of his glory." . . . Then I heard the voice of the Lord saying, "Whom shall I send? And who will go for us?" *And I said, "Here am I. Send me!"* (Isaiah 6:3, 8 NIV, emphasis added)

ACKNOWLEDGEMENTS

First of all, all glory to God! I pray this book is pleasing to Him. May I continue to say, "Here I am, send me."

This book has been years in the making. It has been an incredible learning experience. As with my first book, I have sought to be real and raw. I wrote this one because of what took place with my first one, opening doors and getting to hear other peoples' stories. It is impossible to include them all, but if I've heard your story, it is etched in my heart and mind and you are part of this book. The prayers, support, encouragement, input, and editing include several family and friends who are dear to me. A heartfelt thanks goes to each one of you!

I would like to take time to thank the book project team as they had one crazy job ahead of them.

My husband, Jim, to whom I dedicate this book. He is all I described in the dedication and more. I couldn't have written this book without you on so many levels. Thanks to Pastor Ben Poole for your godly wisdom and for authoring a chapter in this book. You understand the Father's love and it is exemplified in your life! Our daughter, Jessica Chew, with her brilliant and creative ways in helping organize the cover. I love that you are part of this book project! You're my "Somewhere Over the Rainbow." Thank you to my cousin, Tim O'Malley, who takes some of the most beautiful photos I've ever seen and for the incredible picture you took of a rainbow in the dark on the cover. Thanks for all your prayers too!

Patricia McClean, my dear friend, who believes in my calling in this project and has spent much time editing it again and again and again. She has continuously prayed, and I've felt those prayers. She wrote, "Faith sustains me when things seem hopeless." She is an author whose upcoming book is one I very much look forward to reading. Heidi Sandler, who is a kind soul and full of wisdom. Thank you for graciously and patiently editing my grammatical messiness! You've helped in numerous ways. Lee Warren, who literally came in on this project at just the right time . . . God's timing. He is extremely gifted and professionally knowledgeable on so many levels. You saved the day! My niece, Valerie Germeroth, who is wise beyond her years and my fellow party-loving planner. Most importantly, your steadfast faith. Thanks for seeing if this would minister to high school level students too! Rita Sutton, who offered great feedback. You've always been so caring! I appreciate your godly insight! Kelly Sullivan, I so miss you being our neighbor! One of the sweetest people I know and intelligent. Thanks for all your input! Thanks to my cheerleaders, Karen Shappei Maxwell and Tammy Kowalski Henson for being my promoters for my first book and now this one, even when I don't do PR! You kept me going on this project.

And last but not least, I'm thankful for my parents who have prayed for us daily and often! In memory of my dad, who sadly didn't get to see the final product but is with our Loving Father. Thank you to our kids, who I can't be more proud of as they make such an impact for God's kingdom and inspire me daily. And I prayed, as I wrote this book, that our grandchildren would read it someday and see beyond the circumstances and how God is truly Our Rainbow in the Dark.

AUTHOR BIO

Colleen's greatest desire is to serve God and serve Him well. This is why Isaiah 6:8 is her life verse.

She enjoys connecting with her readers through real-life adventures and experiences. She hopes to encourage others, explaining that God's grace is sufficient and that He is all. Her first book, *The Raindrops on the Windshield*, has been read by readers around the world, including India, Africa, Poland, Canada, and here in the United States. This experience opened doors for her to become a national and international speaker. She has loved meeting people and hearing their stories, which prompted her to write *A Rainbow in the Dark*.

Colleen has been dating her hot and humble husband since 1986, starting at a 1980s video dance. Their adult children and sweet grandchildren continue to provide the greatest joys in life and inspire Colleen daily.

Before she started writing books, Colleen received her master's degree in art therapy. She continues to study neuroscience and is an international crisis therapist, life coach, and professor.

Please feel free to contact Colleen at https://www.realandrawministry.org or blueprint4u@gmail.com.

Made in the USA
Columbia, SC
19 July 2022

63717221R00098